THE ILLUMINATION CODEX
GATEWAY THREE

PATH OF AWAKENING

KEYS FOR TRANSFIGURATION

MICHAEL GARBER

MICHAEL GARBER

Printed in the United States of America
First Printing 2021
First Edition 2021

Second Edition

ISBNs:
Softcover 978-1-959561-11-8
eBook 978-1-959561-12-5

10 9 8 7 6 5 4 3 2 1

THE ILLUMINATION CODEX

Table of Contents

ACKNOWLEDGMENTS

I bow in humble recognition of the One Light of Consciousness, the Source of my being and the source of all knowledge and wisdom. I give gratitude to the Supreme for dreaming me into existence and allowing me to have the conscious experience of life and the crafting of this codex.

I bow in love and gratitude to my dear beloved partner Ron Amit, a true gift of the Divine, for all the many ways he supports me in my life. I am blessed beyond measure to have such a brilliant master of love, compassion, and divine service to walk this earthly life with. Thank you for all that you do, seen and unseen, to amplify joy and higher consciousness for me and all beings in the Cosmos. I love you across all space, time, and dimensions.

I send gratitude to my friends and clients who have brought forth the lost stories of Creation through their Illuminated Quantum Healing hypnosis sessions. Thank you for being the powerful Light beacons that you are!

I send deep gratitude to my many modern scribes who assisted me in the transcription work. Thank you for helping me capture these incredible client stories so that the world can remember our cosmic divine heritage.

Bless all the beings, seen and unseen, who have helped me craft this material so that you, the reader, can be nourished on your path of Ascension. May you, the reader, be blessed infinitely and discover the highest truth of your being. May ascended consciousness, liberation, and divine unification be yours in this very life!

DEDICATION AND INVOCATION

This book is dedicated to the infinite expressions of our Oneself, for the celebration of our many incarnations, past, present, and future, and the lessons we have learned throughout eternity. May these words and the energy they carry be a potent force for awakening for all seekers of Unconditional Love and divine Truth. May this transmission support the reactivation and restoration of humanity's divine blueprint upon planet Earth and accelerate the realization of our eternal unity and oneness with all of Creation.

Let us join in prayer, honoring and sending gratitude to the Supreme Intelligent Source of Creation, the omniscient, omnipotent, omnipresent, transcendental Divine Source that is our True Nature.

Let us honor and send gratitude to the higher Light realms and the beings of Light who guide and protect Creation's evolution. Let us honor and send gratitude to our star lineages and those who support us from beyond the Earth. Let us receive your love and blessings now as we remember our cosmic ancestry and our role in the higher evolutionary plan for Creation.

Let us honor and send gratitude to our Earth Mother and her many dimensions and manifestations of Life including the animal, plant, bacterial, fungal, protozoan, mineral, crystalline, and elemental beings who contribute to her dynamic, regenerative biomes. These writings are offered as salve and balm to heal and bless our beloved Gaia, our Earth Mother and Divine Sister. May her waters be pure, her soil rich, her air clean, and may all beings, seen and unseen, within her living biofield know lasting peace forever and ever.

Let us honor and send gratitude to the wisdom and guidance from the seven directions of East, South, West, North, Above, Below, and Within. Let us call back our soul fragments scattered through time and space so that we may anchor ourselves HERE and NOW in this eternal moment of infinite potential to witness the unfolding manifestation of the Divine Plan.

Let us honor and send gratitude to the elements of Earth, Air, Fire, Water, and Ether that create the foundation of our evolutionary experience in form. May the Light of Consciousness awaken swiftly in each of us as we remember our True Nature beyond names and forms.

Let us honor and send gratitude to our ancestors and the many souls who have shared their light upon the Earth. Let us send special thanks to those who dedicated their lives to passing on the Mysteries and sacred knowledge of the Divine so that we may NOW stand at this Grand Turning of the Ages, with the support of all who have come and all who are destined to live upon this great Earth.

I call forth the full remembering of our divinity and the weaving of a new story of harmony and peace for all of Life upon the Earth. May we shed our stories of limitation and suffering and step forward into a new era as People of Light, cosmic co-citizens, and ambassadors for the Living Light of Creation.

Hallelujah! Jai! Aho! Blessed Be! Amen! And so, it is! Om!

GUIDANCE FOR READING THIS BOOK

The Illumination Codex is a multidimensional library for the path of Ascension. It is holographic by nature as each chapter contains a multitude of keycodes to activate ancient cellular memory and trigger multidimensional awareness and higher consciousness integration. As you read the material, your Inner Being will offer flashes of insight and higher perception into your awareness to assist you in healing, spiritual activation, and cosmic remembrance. I recommend using a highlighter, journaling your process, and using other resources to research and enhance your understanding of the topics presented in this book.

A major influence for this material comes from my work as a past-life regression hypnotherapist using the methods we have codified into a technique called Illuminated Quantum Healing (IQH). While in a deep hypnotic trance, my clients experience other lifetimes and other planetary civilizations and communicate with advanced intelligent species from beyond the Earth and Earth plane. The information contained in this book is a summary of my understanding of all that I have learned through my clients as they journeyed to the ancient past, probable timelines of the future, and higher planes of Light. There are many transcriptions of IQH sessions included in the book for you to have your own unique interpretation and multidimensional experience with the material.

This book contains a diverse collection of spiritual information from a variety of wisdom traditions that I have studied in my life. These writings are my own interpretations and understandings of these different concepts that have helped me in my awakening journey and do not necessarily speak for the lineages themselves. This presentation of information is meant as a collection of keys to unlock the wisdom that is already encoded within you. None of it is meant to become dogmatic as consciousness revelation and ascendency will open us continuously to higher and higher truths and understanding.

I confess that I share this transmission as a fellow traveler on the path of awakening. I have my own limitations, my own egoic nature, and my own struggles. I am capable of error and ignorance just as any other person. This presentation of information is what I have found along my path which has triggered awakening and helped me on my path back home to my Self. My prayer is that this book will become deeply meaningful for you and be a guiding light back to your own liberated being.

While reading this material, you may come across something in the text that triggers something within you that is uncomfortable. Maybe it is words that I use, perspectives that I share, or something else that may bring up resistance, judgment, anger, guilt, and so on. This is a wonderful opportunity to investigate the origin of the reactive mental and emotional patterns that create such experiences. The origin may come from earlier stages of your life or previous lifetimes. Use this as an opportunity to reconcile those parts of your consciousness through spiritual inquiry and self-study so that you may realize deeper states of wholeness and clarity.

This text is intended to activate 'gnosis,' a direct experience and knowledge of the divine presence within and around you. I do not recommend blind faith in any concept or religious doctrine. The information in this book is not meant to be treated as religious dogma that cannot be questioned or developed further. It is meant to be utilized to unlock the truth that lives within your very being. I am not writing this intending to change people's beliefs or convert anyone. I am simply relaying the summary of my life's research on the quest for spiritual truth. If something from the material does not resonate as truth in your heart, release it and move on to the next part of the transmission. Use the philosophy and information in this text to stimulate your expansion and the embodiment of YOUR deepest truth and to strengthen your relationship and innate connection with the Divine.

Another thing to mention is capitalization. You will notice that there are words that are not normally capitalized in other books and sacred texts that are capitalized in this text. My intention behind this was to add spiritual dimensionality to words that describe qualities or names of the Divine.

Typically, when I speak of light in this book, I am speaking about higher-dimensional, intelligently-encoded subtle energy and not conventional light from a light bulb. When I speak about "energy," I am speaking about subtle energy which exists beyond the visible light spectrum for most people. Many are becoming sensitive to subtle energy (i.e., multisensory, intuitive, psychic) and are developing the ability to sense and perceive this energy through extrasensory perception. All of humanity is evolving towards being able to perceive and interact with subtle energy and higher cosmic intelligence and consciousness.

The use of the term consciousness fluctuates throughout the book and can mean different things. When I speak of pure Consciousness I am speaking about your True Self as Source Consciousness, the Absolute, the Eternal Witness of all Creation, pure Awareness and Existence itself. Other times I will speak of consciousness as in variations of the mind such as unity consciousness or separation consciousness. All forms of consciousness, all experiences of the mind, borrow existence from the One Light of Consciousness and you are that!

I tried my best to organize this text in a way that can be read from front to back like any regular book, but it can also be read any way you feel intuitively called to read it. Part of the reason for the size of this codex is because it is difficult to explain one part without understanding many other components. In my effort to answer all potential and probable questions about ascension, I wrote everything I could on this multifaceted, multidimensional topic.

As you make your journey through this material, there are three stages to help integrate the information and use it to fuel your awakening to your True Nature:

Stage One: Listening (*Sravana*) As you read or listen to the material in this book, allow it to penetrate deeply and work with your inner philosophical understanding. Listen deeply to your Inner Being for there will be flashes of insight and knowing that emerge within your inner consciousness space.

Stage Two: Reflection (*Manana*) Try your best to understand the information contained in this book through self-inquiry and inner philosophical pondering. I am not asking for you to blindly believe any of this transmission. Think of this information as an active hypothesis. You do not have to believe it, but you can reflect over the information and see how it applies to your life.

Stage Three: Integration/Meditation (*Nididhyasana*) As you take in the words in stage one and convert the words to knowledge and understanding in stage two, you move into conviction and integration of knowledge in stage three as you crystallize and embody the Self-knowledge of "I am Pure Consciousness." As you go about your daily life, use the knowledge you have gained to interrupt habit and conditioned thought and re-direct your mind toward the Light of Consciousness that you are.

Gateways of Entry

Besides reading front-to-back or intuitively hopping around, I have created six gateways for you to enter the presentation of the material. I have created one large book that has all of the Illumination Codex material and separated the material into separately published volumes to make the information more digestible. The Gateways are as follows:

GATEWAY ONE: ASCENSION INITIATION: KEYS FOR HIGHER EVOLUTION gives an overall understanding of Ascension, reincarnation, universal law, and a theoretical and philosophical framework concerning Cosmic Evolution. This is an excellent place to start if you are open and eager to learn about these subjects and awakening, you may want to start in Gateway Three.

GATEWAY TWO: AKASHIC DATABASE contains a wide variety of Illuminated Quantum Healing session transcriptions describing key figures and events in the history of Creation, galactic history, ancient planetary history, and probable future timelines of New Earth from clients in hypnotic visionary states. This is a suitable place to enter the material if you already have a general understanding of multidimensionality, galactic civilizations, and the process of personal and planetary ascension. This gateway is conveniently separated into QUANTUM ORIGINS, COSMIC CHRIST TRANSMISSIONS, and NEW EARTH TRANSMISSIONS. If you find yourself resistant to those ideas and are new to these subjects. I recommend developing a meditation practice parallel to reading this material as the transcripts are deeply activating on multiple levels.

GATEWAY THREE: PATH OF AWAKENING: KEYS FOR TRANSFIGURATION is an in-depth collection of spiritual and philosophical wisdom to support personal, relational, and planetary healing. If you are in the beginning stages of awakening or moving through a deep healing process, you may wish to start here so you can develop your consciousness and prepare your mind and body for higher level initiation into the Mysteries.

GATEWAY FOUR: CHAKRA YOGA DISCOURSE transmits deeper

insight into the themes and physio-psycho-spiritual domains of the vortices of life force and perception called the *chakras*. Each section transmits valuable information to understand the common distortions in these processing centers and how to activate and reconcile each center.

GATEWAY FIVE: LAYING HANDS: REIKI & BEYOND is a full manual for learning the art of the laying of hands for healing. The manual clearly describes all the stages, steps, and practices to perform powerfully transformative hands-on-healing sessions for yourself, others, and even in groups. This manual would be acceptable for any Level 1 and Level 2 Reiki course.

GATEWAY SIX: ASCENSION LEXICON is a glossary of commonly used words to describe the process of awakening and ascension. These definitions act as keycode activators to unlock deeper meaning and inner wisdom. Many words used in spiritual/ascension circles are convoluted and sometimes lose their impact because they are misused or misunderstood. I may use words in a way you are not familiar with, or I may use words differently than you. I tried my best to make a glossary with foundational vocabulary to assist with understanding the material. You may wish to read the ASCENSION LEXICON before journeying through the main text of the book.

Bless you on your personal path through this material. May the light in your heart guide you with ease and grace on your journey of initiation with *The Illumination Codex.*

ABOUT THE AUTHOR
Awakening to the Quantum Reality

In the Summer of 2016, I was given a book that forever changed my life's direction called *The Three Waves of Volunteers and the New Earth* by Dolores Cannon. This book was a huge catalyst in my spiritual awakening. Reading the text stirred something deep within me and resonated profoundly with my heart's truth. The book's pages sent waves of energy down my spine as I began to awaken to a higher consciousness reality and remember my purpose for being born upon the Earth at this time.

Dolores Cannon was a world-renowned hypnotherapist specializing in past-life regression. To understand the power of regressive hypnosis, we also need to understand the workings of the mind. The mind can be separated into three categories: the conscious mind, the subconscious mind, and the superconscious mind.

The conscious mind is the ego/personality part of the mind. This active part of the mind uses limited information from the environment and past experiences to make decisions and take care of the body.

The subconscious mind is the recording device of our mind. It records incredible amounts of information at every moment. We easily pull data from the subconscious when we think about something from our past as we access memory.

Deeper in the subconscious, sometimes called the unconscious mind, we have unconscious memories and information, including societal conditioning, painful traumas from this life that are too painful to remember, and memories from other lifetimes. Even though this information is not in the conscious mind, it silently influences our day-to-day experience as reactive emotional momentum, called *samskaras* in Sanskrit, from past events which overlay and filter our experience of the present moment. These subconscious patterns are like applications running in the background of smartphones that quietly drain the processing speed and battery, silently influencing processor speed and functionality.

The superconscious mind is a higher mind capacity that gives us access to intuitive information, extrasensory perception, non-local consciousness, creative genius, universal connection, and access to divine consciousness. This part of the mind is mostly undiscovered and underdeveloped in most of humanity.

Dolores created a unique method of hypnosis, Quantum Healing Hypnosis Technique (QHHT), that opened a doorway to the client's subconscious mind to explore other lifetimes and realms in Creation. When I use the word "quantum," I am speaking to the fabric of Consciousness, the multidimensional unified field of Creation. When clients are in these hypnotic states, they tap into the part of their consciousness that is nonlocal and connected to All That Is. This includes access to other lifetimes, other realities and dimensions, and other intelligent consciousness forms (i.e., higher-dimensional light beings, telepathic extraterrestrials, etc.). Through this experience, clients came to understand another perspective and origin of self-sabotaging and limiting beliefs that were playing out in this life and the core mental/emotional patterns that create illness and disease.

During her sessions, Dolores started to contact a part of her clients' consciousness that seemed to have endless knowledge and wisdom. She called this aspect of her clients the Subconscious or the SC. Others have called this the Higher Self, the oversoul, superconsciousness, or the cosmic consciousness. I prefer the term Higher Self and superconscious mind and go into great detail of how to activate and evolve superconsciousness throughout this text. While the information was limitless, the SC/Higher Self would only answer questions in a way that was appropriate for the client's learning path and honored their free will. When working with the SC, both Dolores and the client described powerful healing energy in their bodies and the treatment room. Clients often reported instantaneous healing as they were transformed from the inside out during the session. While this may seem too good to be true, there are countless documented and measurable occurrences where clients received lasting miraculous healing through these types of sessions.

When she would work with the Higher Self, this higher consciousness identity and supportive Light team would speak through the client as a collective consciousness as if the client were speaking in third-person perspective about themselves. "We are always guiding her. We wish she would follow her intuition more." and "We are beginning to use white light to heal this now." are common examples of how "They" (i.e., SC/Higher Self) express themselves and heal the client during the session.

The healing work is always done with unconditional love and honors the free will and sovereignty of the client. If instantaneous healing was not "appropriate" for the client's growth and spiritual maturation, "They" would suggest what steps the client should take to heal themselves. Slowly, over many years, Dolores's work expanded as "They" introduced more components to the healing process so that she could evolve her work and teach it to others.

The Three Waves of Volunteers and the New Earth was one of nineteen books written by Dolores Cannon before her transition out of physical life. Each book contains transcriptions of client sessions describing detailed events from other lives while using her Quantum Healing Hypnosis Technique (QHHT).

Awakening to the Starseed Volunteer Mission

After several years of working with clients worldwide, Dolores noticed a pattern of clients describing a massive galactic and higher dimensional mission to raise the vibration of the planet and shift it into a new reality called the New Earth. The book describes how countless numbers of advanced spiritual beings from distant star systems, and even other universes, volunteered to incarnate on the Earth with a mission to raise consciousness on the planet and assist with this grand transition.

The New Earth is a higher frequency Earth reality that exists in a higher dimension than we are in now. Clients describe a large-scale plan initiated by Source Intelligence (God) to reset life on planet Earth back to the original template of a harmonic environment thriving within diversity. Parallel to this, Dolores's work described a shift in human consciousness from a duality-based mindset to a heart-centered, multidimensional consciousness and a less physical body of light.

The First Wave Volunteers were born beginning around 1945 through the 1970s. They were like a stealthy reconnaissance mission. First on the scene. First to patrol and feel out the collective consciousness vibrations. First to introduce the higher consciousness perspectives to the masses. Many had a difficult and lonely time since there were not many other humans in higher, love-based spiritual consciousness on the planet at the time.

The Second Wave Volunteers were born around the late 1970s through

1990s and are channels for higher spiritual energy and divine wisdom. These souls came in with a higher level of intuitive gifts and are often extremely sensitive to energy. Many are hands-on healers, musicians, vocalists, yoga teachers, and so on. They are space-holders who transmit a new frequency out to the field of Earth, bridging the old ways with the new ways and consciousness of New Earth.

The Third Wave Volunteers, the younger generations, are builders and innovative geniuses in science, spirituality, technology, and so on. They are divinely inspired visionaries that will build the New Earth. They are radical lovers and shine bright with crystalline eyes and have achieved high consciousness levels in other lifetimes. Some of these souls have never had a physical incarnation or have come straight from Source as new souls with pure Light and no karma.

I have been told all the children born at this time are part of this Grand Mission. They are pure souls, evolutionary masters, here to build the New Earth. More is written about the Starseed Mission and phenomena later in this book.

As I was reading Dolores's book, I felt I was reading my own story. I felt the truth in her words. Suddenly so many things made sense about my life. I finally had answers to why I felt so different from others in my community and family. I understood why I felt other people's emotions and could tell what people were thinking. It all started to click together. I was so excited to share the book with Ron, my husband and co-founder of New Earth Ascending, who also deeply resonated with the material.

At the same time, we were beginning to work with an Australian musical group as dancers for their "Return of the Bird Tribes" tour for their album by the same name. Something about the term "bird tribes" caught my attention, and I started to research it. I found the book by the same name, written by Ken Carey, in 1988 that describes a prophecy of high spiritual beings returning to the Earth at a time of spiritual renewal.

Many cultures describe times when culture-bringing beings would come from the heavens or from across the waters to bring technology and information to humanity throughout history. Thoth went to the Egyptians, White Buffalo Calf Woman went to the Native Americans, Quetzalcoatl went to the Aztecs, the Seven Sisters of the Pleiades went to the Aboriginal people of Australia, beings from the Sirius A and B binary star system went to the Dogon people of Mali; and many other stories exist in many other cultures. Carey's book described when these beings would come again during a time of spiritual awakening on the planet.

I was receiving information from multiple directions and was going through a massive realignment with my soul's purpose as I became aware of this greater story and mission. Ron and I went to an arts festival in the desert of Nevada called Burning Man. While we were there, a couple excitedly recognized us as "twin flames" and asked us which star system we had come from. "We are from Sirius. Where are you from? Orion? The Pleiades? Sirius?" she asked. The concept of "starseeds" and "twin flames" was new to me, and I did not know what to say. I saw a special sparkle in the couple's eyes and felt that I should do some research to understand more about it.

After some research and some magical synchronicities, Ron convinced me that we should do the QHHT training and certification process. I was super resistant to learning it because of deep religious programming and egoic structures that made me doubtful of the truthfulness of the work. I was familiar with reincarnation but did not necessarily believe in it. Eventually, I gave in to Ron's suggestion and took the QHHT course.

Evolving Beyond QHHT

In the early stages of practicing QHHT, Ron and I were guided to start doing the sessions online to share the technique's power with as many people as we could. This method was not permitted by the organization because Dolores did not believe it to be safe and her organization does not permit it still. Dolores was an elder and this type of technology was new to her, whereas the younger generations are much more comfortable interfacing with video conferencing.

We have been told by the Higher Consciousness that there is nothing to fear, and NOW is the time to spread these healing methods across the world in whatever way is possible. To honor our lineage and teacher, we stopped using the name QHHT and started experimenting with different names as our way of practicing quantum healing evolved beyond our initial training.

Online sessions are just as powerful as in-person sessions and are often more comfortable and affordable for the client. It is completely safe to facilitate sessions remotely, and we have had countless powerful sessions that have been facilitated in this way. Dolores's organization does not allow adaptation of the QHHT technique. Its practitioners need to perform the method exactly how Dolores taught and not add any modifications or outside techniques. While it is important to protect the work's integrity, this rigidity does not permit the work to expand to its full potential. We are in a time of expansion and evolution, and we must always be open to the transformation and progression of all methods we currently use or risk leaving them in the past as everything on the Earth is evolving.

Another topic that caused us to evolve beyond our initial training of QHHT was the organization's strict denial of negative spiritual attachment and what felt like shaming those who believed in this common experience. Ron and I and other quantum healing practitioners discovered that certain psychological, emotional, and physical imbalances were being created by pervasive energies that did not belong to the client's energy field that had somehow become attached to the client. This includes spirit attachments, curses from past lives, and implants from nefarious beings to name a few. QHHT did not provide us with appropriate training to work with these serious complications. If it were found out that a practitioner had adopted these practices and still operated under the name of QHHT, practitioners could be removed from the QHHT directory.

Many practitioners have reported spontaneous visitation from Dolores through clients under hypnosis where she has encouraged practitioners to follow their intuitive guidance and continue to develop the work through experimentation just as she did when she developed QHHT.

We were inspired greatly by other quantum healing practitioners' extraction methods and crafted our own approaches to clearing pervasive energies and spirit attachments. The reality of negative thought-forms, negative extraterrestrial implants, and entity attachment is too big to ignore, considering so many cases are emerging, not to forget the thousands of years of wisdom and extraction practices passed down by Indigenous peoples and various wisdom traditions.

We never assume that someone has an entity just because they suffer, and we do not bring it up in our intake interview. Once the client is deep in a hypnotic trance, we ask the Higher Self if there are entities or attached energies. If the answer is yes, then we ask questions to understand how this occurred and if the client has anything to learn to release negative attachment. From there, the Higher Self can immediately extract the energy and take it back into the Light for healing. It is all extremely safe, insightful, and benefits all who are involved. We have found that, often, the revelation of spirit attachment or implants will not occur unless the practitioner asks and gives permission for a scan specifically for attached energies. Ron and I believe this is because of the honoring of the free will of the entities involved in the experience of attachment.

In my opinion, to continue to deny such experiences is a disservice to the clients who come to us seeking answers and healing. All practices and traditions can become dogmatic if we do not allow the evolution of thought to take us into new frontiers of consciousness. These are evolutionary practices, and we need to be constantly open to shifting our paradigm so that we can offer the best guidance and support with the changing of times.

Once we started offering quantum healing sessions online, clients started coming to Ron and me from all over the world. Not only were the sessions powerfully healing and transformative for the clients, but we were also going through a rapid transformation as we learned about ancient stories and galactic events from the perspective of souls embodied at those times. While Dolores taught that many people had "potato-picking lives," simple lives with simple themes, it seemed that almost every session of mine had to do with the New Earth Mission, powerful events from the ancient past, and future timelines of Earth.

I soon realized that I was getting a theme and timeline in my sessions. The timeline given to me via my clients describes how Creation came into being, ancient galactic history, the seeding of life on Earth, the rise and fall of ancient civilizations, the true teachings of Jesus through the eyes of people that were closest to him, information about the transformation of the human body to a less dense body of Light, and the evolution of the Earth into the higher frequency reality of New Earth. In less than a year, I went from a reincarnation skeptic to believing that anything is possible, and that the multiverse is more incredible than we can even imagine!

Illuminated Quantum Healing

After years of practicing and evolving how we do this work, Ron and I have created our own quantum healing method that incorporates all that we have learned on our path. This includes facilitating sessions online to reach as many people as possible to assist in this Great Awakening.

Our training method acknowledges spirit attachment and teaches our facilitators how to perform negative spirit releasement. We teach yogic psychology, holistic wellness concepts, and energy healing methods to ensure the practitioner has a thorough understanding of human consciousness and how to lead the client through the ascension process using multiple IQH sessions and mentorship programs. We call our method Illuminated Quantum Healing. IQH can be learned in live classes or through our online course offered on our social network Source⊙Energy.

Illuminated Quantum Healing (IQH) is a personal transformation method for multidimensional holistic healing and consciousness development. IQH incorporates energy healing, meditative practices, yogic philosophy, and hypnosis skills to reconcile limiting subconscious patterning and integrate instantaneous multidimensional healing and wisdom from one's Higher Self.

I am deeply honored to be a part of this work. I am so blessed to have an opportunity to work with such incredible people and energies. Each session that I facilitate nourishes me to the core, and I have the sublime opportunity to observe miraculous instantaneous healing and transformation in my clients. After witnessing the infinite potential of quantum healing hypnosis, I firmly believe that we can ascend beyond all states of illness and disease and that we have infinite support to move beyond the shadows of our past and become a new People of Light.

Getting to the New Earth involves a process of spiritual growth and purification. To transition with the Earth, it is required that we raise our vibration to match the accelerating frequency of the Earth as it changes. Mostly, this is about releasing fear and negative karma. I have written this book as a tool to use for your spiritual awakening and transformation that many are calling Ascension. This is my gift to humanity to help make the process easier and explain different components to cultivate a deeper understanding of this Grand Shift to New Earth and our newly evolving Lightbody.

Spiritual awakening and ascension are available for ALL people no matter what they have done in their past, current economic status, gender expression, sexuality, religion, etc. There are as many paths to the New Earth as there are humans on the planet. No one religion holds the keys or the way to heaven. The power is within YOU!

To support the global ascension process, we have created New Earth Ascending. New Earth Ascending is a non-profit, faith-based organization focused on global ascension and establishing heart-centered, sustainable communities and educational centers around the world.

Alongside Illuminated Quantum Healing (IQH), Ron and I have created other pathways of support for the global ascension process:

1. Embodied Light Reiki Training and Certification

2. New Earth Ascending has three levels of Reiki certification to train people how to channel divine light for healing. These trainings honor the lineage and teachings of the Usui System of Natural Healing while also infusing evolutionary concepts and practices that go beyond standard Reiki training.

3. Online courses for awakening and ascension are available on our private social network Source⊙Energy. The courses include philosophical exploration on several models of spiritual growth and alchemical practices to support your healing, awakening, and ascension. These courses include meditations, holistic wellness education, breathwork, lightbody activation and more. These courses lay foundational understanding for beginners and move through a progression of intermediate and advanced practices and knowledge.

4. TransformOtion was created to support the embodiment of one's Higher Self using dance, somatic movement, yogic practices, meditation, imagination, and energy healing. This fusion of practices helps to purify and repair the physical, etheric, and mental bodies so that one can move beyond perceived limitations into boundless rhythm and flow. Through this interweaving of multiple disciplinary paths, we integrate physicality with transcendental ecstatic play while cultivating a deep connection with and trust in the body's wisdom.

These ideas and concepts can be used for personal embodiment and activation or infused into performance art to create powerful alchemical experiences for the performer and the audience. This fusion of high art and spiritual transformation creates a multidimensional experience for all who are within the field of performance energies.

5. Source⊙Energy is a social network exclusively for those on the path of ascension to connect and share inspiration as we manifest and build a New Earth. We invite all souls who feel aligned with New Earth to join this network and add your unique energy and love to this community. Source⊙Energy serves as a pathway of social interaction and is the home of our online courses and training.

6. Children are our future. Youth inspiration and enrichment programming is in development to assist the spiritual activation and consciousness mastery of the youth. NEA is dedicated to creating harmonic environments and rich educational programs to guide youth to connect with cosmic intelligence and embody their divine nature and mastery as they build the New Earth.

Ron and I have dedicated our lives to supporting this Grand Transition. We stand alongside all of you as humanity awakens to its True Nature and becomes a People of Light in the heavenly reality of New Earth.

New Earth Ascending is dedicated to assisting people to realize their divinity and manifest that truth in every aspect of their life. For more information about New Earth Ascending or to contact Michael, please scan the QR code below for a list of resources and links, or visit _www.newearthascending.org_. Be sure to check out our courses including the Illuminated Quantum Healing practitioner course.

New Earth Ascending is a registered 508 (c)(1)(a) Self-Supported Non-profit Church Ministry with a global outreach. We greatly appreciate your support as we create new systems, communities, and schools for the development of the New Earth civilization. If you would like to make a tax-deductible donation to support our mission, please go to:

https://donorbox.org/donationtonewearthascending

Scan with a smart device camera for more information!

NEW EARTH ASCENDING VISIONARY CREED

We acknowledge the sovereignty and equality of all levels of Creation and support the liberation of all of Life from cycles of suffering. We believe in the power of divine sovereign creatorship endowed to us by God/Source and dedicate our life to Light and Love in service to All. We believe in conscious participation, empowering everyone to activate awakening in themselves and their community.

We recognize free will and surrender our will and desires to the higher will of the Divine. We believe in divine timing and practice trust, patience, and tolerance as we witness the unfoldment of the perfection of the Divine Plan. We believe in the potency of empowering prayer, meditation, and ritual as tools for communication with the Divine for the culmination of spiritual light and divine wisdom. We believe everyone has a direct connection to the Source and no intermediary is needed. When we come together in fellowship, prayer, and devotion, we amplify the light of each individuals' loving intention through our unified, heart-centered consciousness.

We seek to uplift all groups and communities so that we may celebrate our unity, diversity, and wholeness. New Earth Ascending is non-competitive and embraces an ecumenical relationship with all religions and wisdom traditions. We believe in interfaith and inter-spirituality, acknowledging the teachings of Light, Love, and Wisdom in many traditions, philosophies, and cultures. We believe that no single religion holds the keys to the Kingdom of God and the blessings of redemption are available to all people through their unbreakable innate connection to the Godhead.

We believe in the Law of Oneness and that all of Creation emanates from one Divine Source that has both masculine and feminine principles. As we heal and balance the divine masculine and divine feminine principles within us, we embody the divine androgyny of Source and Nature as a harmonic synthesis of Spirit and Matter.

We believe that humanity and planet Earth are going through a rapid physical and spiritual transformation called by many as The Ascension or The Event. We believe this process to be part of a higher evolutionary divine plan guided by the Source of Creation and legions of beings working for the Light. This evolutionary process is multidimensional and is beyond the standard biological evolution spoken of by modern science.

We believe that we, as humanity, are awakening to our spiritual Self and are becoming a heart-based, unity-focused species with higher, multidimensional awareness, which some call Christ Consciousness, Cosmic Consciousness, or 5D Consciousness. We believe this transformation's power is happening through our divinely designed and curated DNA as the physical body transforms into a less dense body of Light with tremendously expanded multidimensional abilities.

We believe that Planet Earth, the sentient being of Gaia, is going through a similar restoration process and will soon transform into a revitalized higher dimensional planet, which many are calling the New Earth. Earth changes, weather events, crumbling institutional structures, frequency fluctuations, and astrological phenomena are all signs that we are nearing that shift into the next Golden Age, where Heaven and Earth become one and all systems of control and limitation will fall away.

We believe that we are supported by benevolent higher dimensional, subterranean, and extraterrestrial beings that work in harmonic collaboration with the higher evolutionary Divine Plan of Source. We believe that soon humanity will be consciously reunited with these benevolent beings and serve the higher evolutionary plan of the Light and Love of Source as cosmic co-citizens of the Multiverse working as one Family of Light in service to all of Creation.

We understand that the pathway of Self/Source-Realization and Ascension is comprised of self-study, self-practice, self-discipline, and steadfastness. We practice self-care and self-purification to clarify our Light. We acknowledge and value the acceleration of this process when we practice together in groupings of two or more in fellowship and worship.

We strive to grow in awareness and focused attention, practicing mindfulness in all areas of our lives to grow as conscious, heart-centered creators. We choose to focus our life positively with faith and knowing that Life is evolving in perfection following the Divine Plan of the Supreme Source.

We believe in the power of intention. We practice nonviolence and non-harmfulness in intention, thought, and action. We strive to release all forms of judgment and dual thinking. We honor the sacred heart's radiant potential and believe loving compassion and understanding to be The Way. We practice the heart-centered qualities of gentleness, reverence, loving-kindness, and forgiveness as pathways to reconciliation to emulate the eternal grace of Source and our Earth Mother, Gaia.

We see that Truth is alive within each of us, and we practice inner reflection to grow in discernment for what energies are resonant with our inner Source and our path. We practice benevolent truthfulness, honesty, straightforwardness, and vulnerability to embody and vocalize our deepest truth.

We value and practice transparency and accountability, believing in the opportunity for spiritual growth through spiritual partnership with our community members. We recognize one another as divine mirrors, reflecting to us where we are in our vibration, beliefs, and intentions.

We practice sacred sexuality as an alchemical tool for Divine Union and Ascension. We strive to purify our intentions and desires to align with Higher Love and authentic connection. We believe in heart-based self and consensual mutual pleasure to unite body, mind, and spirit so that we may deepen in our love and authentic connection to our Divine Self, our partner(s), and Creation.

We practice contentment, acceptance, appreciation, and gratitude for our life's many blessings and lessons. We practice non-attachment, non-possessiveness, non-stealing, non-excess, and sustainability, for all we need is given to us through our alignment with our Creator Source and our connection to our Earth Mother. We practice stewardship and sustainable selfless service, acknowledging our responsibility to take care of the world around us and within.

We practice sacred commerce, investing our resources, time, and energy towards the greater good and sustainability of our community and planet. We believe in reciprocal energy exchange and strive to do so when able. We practice generosity, hospitality, and charitability as reflections of the abundance of the Universe.

We strive to embody and emulate these spiritual principles to manifest the complete liberation of all beings from cycles of suffering and to assist this Grand Transition into the New Earth.

Bless us all!

GATEWAY THREE:
PATH OF AWAKENING

Keys for Transfiguration

This transmission is a library of information to help you on your path of awakening, healing, and Lightbody ascension. I will describe the ascending pathway out the shadowy depths of suffering and distortion so that you may emerge into the blissful and joyful unification with your True Nature. May these pages help illuminate the path of your exodus from bondage and suffering into the promised land of liberation, abundance, and lasting peace!

ONE

Path of Illumination

OM Lead us from the unreal to the Real
From darkness unto Light
From the illusion of death to the truth of immortality
OM Peace! Peace! Peace!
—English translation of the Pavamana Mantra

Everyone has their own unique definition of what spirituality is and what spiritual awakening means and entails. For me, spiritual awakening is about moving from spiritual ignorance into higher truths and higher consciousness. It is about doing shadow work to illuminate and integrate subconscious patterning that obscures my access to joy or causes suffering for myself or anything else. It is about learning the truth of who I am as an eternal, infinite being of divine light and facing all of life with increasing faith and consciousness. Spiritual living involves growing in devotion, seeking divine knowledge, living a life of higher altruistic service, and repeatedly bringing my mind to focus on and contemplate the Divine.

Humanity awakens in stages and groups so that those who have experience in the ascension process can share support and wisdom with those who are moving through an earlier stage of the process. With each wave of Light that ripples across our planet, another group of souls begins their awakening process, and another layer of distortion and trauma rises to the surface of our individual and collective awareness to finally be released. Most people will have no idea what is happening to them as they begin to go through their purging and healing phases and begin to activate spiritually. As they tune into their Inner Being and intuitive intelligence guidance system, they will be led to information sources to help them.

There is a saying "you cannot serve mammon and God," meaning you cannot serve the selfishness and greed of this world and simultaneously serve the higher will of your Divine Nature. Spiritual awakening is a radical act of rebellion because you are inherently detaching from the mainstream culture and walking on a less traveled path. This does not mean that you cannot have and enjoy riches or luxurious experiences. We can use the goals of our life, our desires, possessions, careers, relationships, and all of the other activities to serve our higher dharmic path and live a life of spiritual ethics.

Four *Purusharthas*: Four Goals of Human Life

Before awakening, our life is driven by the conditioning of The World and by our selfish desires. As we awaken, we begin to convert our mentality from "the ways of the world" and turn our focus, will, and intention towards a higher path. It is said in the ancient scriptures that there are four main goals of human life; the four *purusharthas* are:

1. Pursuit of Higher Purpose (*dharma*) — Virtuous path of living one's higher purpose and performing the duties and responsibilities of one's life in accordance with spiritual ethics.
2. Pursuit of Material Prosperity (*artha*) — Acquiring the means and material comforts of life such as a nice home, a good career, and financial security.
3. Pursuit of Happiness and Pleasure (*kama*) — The desire for love, intimacy, pleasure, and affection.
4. Pursuit of Liberation (*moksha*) — God-realization, the highest purpose of human life, said to be achieved when *dharma*, *artha*, and *kama* are achieved and balanced.

Activation of the Mystical Path of Liberation

Before awakening, we are fully invested in the life of the material world, our physical body, and our egoic identity. We are seemingly cut off from everything else and often tormented by cycles of suffering, fear-based lack-consciousness, and victimhood. We are indoctrinated by "The World" through institutions, familial conditioning, and societal conditioning, having taken on their respective limitations, distortions, and control programming.

At some point, a person may look beyond their physicality and limited human identity and become curious and aware of their own essence, their own soul, and how it relates to a Higher Power. A curiosity stirs within their being and the honest seeker sets off on the sacred journey to discover the truth of who they are. It may start with a prayer. It may start with a crisis. It might start with a serendipitous encounter or something else. Whatever it might be, an activation occurs, and the spiritual potential of the initiate begins to stir and rise within their consciousness.

When we start to awaken, we start to move out of the stage of endarkenment where our intellectual understanding of who we are as a limited egoic identity starts to fall apart. Some call this the "dark night of the soul" where the things that used to give us meaning and enjoyment now seem frivolous, unfulfilling, and superficial. People may turn to distractions, substances, and other numbing experiences to avoid confronting this existential crisis. For others, they begin to seek out answers to the questions that are stirring within them. They may even have mystical and synchronistic experiences that start them on a journey of seeking higher philosophical and spiritual truth.

After the endarkenment phase, we begin the self-inquiry process and the quest for higher truth. For some, spiritual awakening is focused on a system of religion where the individual is seen as imperfect and corrupted and union with God can only happen in a heavenly realm. This is the path of blind faith where communication with the Transcendental Divine is done through reading institutionally approved scriptures and enacting prescribed methods of prayer. Devotees must work hard to overcome sin and imperfection to earn their place in the Promised Land. For some, this path is sufficient and brings much joy and relief. Others may find this path heavy and limiting and yearn for something more.

Each religion on the planet is a different school for studying the soul and the Divine. Souls are likely to have been students or devotees in various traditions throughout their many incarnations. There is no one better than another. Even an atheistic life is still serving a higher purpose for a soul. All paths eventually lead to the same Source, and God-realization is available for everyone regardless of their religious affiliation, traditions, and customs.

Another path is the path of spiritual knowledge, investigation, and introspection fueled by psychological and philosophical studies, alchemical spiritual practices, and self-inquiry. This path illuminates what you are and what you are not, what is real and absolute, and what is an illusion, temporal, and untrue. In the pre-awakening and religious path, our mind is externalized, and we look for the keys to salvation outside of us. In the path of knowledge, we detach from the ways of The World and direct our mind inward towards the Light that We Are. We increasingly perform our actions from a place of selfless service, devotion, and altruism as we strive to serve the Divine in All. On this path, we do not have to wait until we die to hopefully get into Heaven. We do not have to live countless lives paying back negative karma. On this path, a dedicated aspirant can achieve union with the Divine in this very life!

As we awaken, we begin to turn our focus inward to our inner realm, to explore the energies of our beingness. Often what we find is a huge mess! Layers upon layers of trauma, limiting beliefs, and a sick body full of density and chemicals. As we begin to clear out the density, we make space for the Pure Light of the Divine to dwell and expand within us.

Spiritual growth is the ingathering of Light within our beingness and body. As we welcome the Light and Wisdom of Source to come into our being and follow the call of our inner Source, every cell begins to transform as everything begins to be renewed by the Light. This desire to "Know Thy Self" moves the consciousness of the person beyond biological evolution and into the Higher Evolution, the alchemy of the soul. Belief in a Higher Power of Love and the willingness to follow Divine Truth has begun to set them free, and a new life begins. This can be called "gnosis" as one begins to directly experience the Mysteries of the Divine in life and one's own being.

When a soul chooses the journey of awakening beyond the mundane and into the mystical, an inner voice of higher reasoning awakens (*ruach*). This voice of reason counsels the consciousness of the seeker through the compassion of the heart. Sometimes it is subtle, and sometimes it is powerful. Nonetheless, the soul is "born again" as it moves from generic human consciousness and begins its Higher Studies of Light, Unconditional Love, and spiritual Wisdom.

Spiritual evolution takes time and space to flourish. Time allows us to feel the experience of growth. Space allows us to reflect on our success and opportunities for refinement. With time and space, you can honor your past experiences and see the value in them. You are no longer a victim of the past and you can begin to see your future as a choice. You begin to notice that your inner world is creating your outer world, and you begin to take authority over your experience. The Fourth Dimension (early awakening) is all about growing in compassion, sovereignty, and cultivating the presence of Inner Light. It is about freeing ourselves from the indoctrination of "The World" and allowing the deeper divine truths to emerge and be embodied.

Holding Space for Self

So rarely do people give themselves time to tune into their inner experience and process the complexity of their emotions, thoughts, and desires. Humanity jumps from one activity to the next, one trauma to the next situation, without deeply observing the energy information from the experience. Our bodies and subconscious mind store it all. Over time we develop aches, pains, illness, and disease as the unprocessed information crystallizes and becomes physical.

Holding space is a term used in spiritual growth and self-development circles that means "to hold suffering in an alchemical container of loving awareness so that it may heal." When we tune into our inner experience, we can observe and transform the stagnant energies and open ourselves to more flow, ease, and joy. We can acknowledge that something from the past hurt us more than we were initially aware of and transform it through loving awareness.

The Four Immeasurables: Virtues of a Divine Heart

The *Four Immeasurables* are sublime states that one can achieve through spiritual practices. Cultivating these qualities brings the initiate out of negatively polarized separation consciousness into heart-centered connection, presence, and expression. These virtues of the heart are essential when holding space for yourself, another being, and The World.

1. *Metta* — Loving-kindness

Translated as unconditional friendship, benevolence, and kind-heartedness, the quality of *metta* is embodied as wishing well for all beings. To grow in *metta* requires us to transform our bitterness into wisdom and all our harshness into gentleness. As we grow in loving-kindness and unconditional friendship with all beings, we become a safe and healing presence for the world's suffering. The quality of *metta* gives us the ability to hold the highest outcome for all beings because we can see beyond the separate self and victim patterns and genuinely express care about the well-being of another.

2. *Karuna* — Compassion

Compassion can be translated to "to suffer with." Meaning, through the empathetic capacity of the heart and psyche, we can feel and relate to another's suffering. Since we know the experience of suffering from our own life experiences, we can relate to another's suffering. Our suffering is their suffering. It takes an open heart to feel and have compassion for the suffering of another.

Compassion creates a bridge between you and another. When we soften into compassion, we come into a deeper understanding of another's suffering because we, too, know the experience of pain. We can relate to the ways we behaved when we were tormented by our emotions and have a deeper understanding of the experience of the other. When we are compassionate, we see beyond the separate self and see our being's interconnectedness with all other beings. When we acknowledge that we are truly One, we become concerned with the suffering of the world and do everything we can to relieve the suffering of others because we know that truly there is no "other."

3. *Mudita* — Empathetic Joy

Mudita is embodied when we find joy in the joy of others. Empathetic joy amplifies the joy and liberated light in another. It starts a chain reaction that is infectious and can spread to the hearts of others. When we cultivate an inner state of compassion (*karuna*) and loving-kindness (*metta*), we can even celebrate the good fortune of those who we see as villains because we can see beyond the victim story and into the deeper truth that we all want to experience joy and liberation. When we celebrate the joy of another, we share in one heart.

4. *Upekkha* — Equanimity

Clear-minded, unshakable awareness that is not affected by the changing conditions of life. As the polarities of perceived loss and gain, praise and criticism, sorrow and happiness, and the need to maintain public reputation dissolve we rest in the perfection of pure awareness.

Equanimity is a quality of consciousness that sees beyond polarity and into the sacredness and higher meaning of all expressions of life. In the cultivation of equanimity, we release the game of valuing any person over another, any race over another, any nation over another. This intention generates a mental calmness as the mind releases the habit and polarity of judgment to truly be an ambassador of peace and restoration.

It is important to emphasize that the purpose of awakening is to liberate yourself and all beings. These sublime qualities are easily practiced towards the ones we have little to no conflict with. These sublime qualities of consciousness are harder to evoke when we succumb to the mind's conditioning and the illusion of a separate self. The villains, tricksters, and tormenters of our life show us where we give power to our conditioned minds.

Holding Space for Others

The intention of communication and relating in the highest form is to assist in relieving the suffering of another. When you hold space for someone else, you create an alchemical container of loving nonjudgmental awareness to witness and validate their experience and support them in transforming their suffering.

For this to happen effectively, the witness must be anchored in compassionate, nondual awareness so that they are not triggered by the emotions and potential projections of the other who is suffering. This requires deep listening within and connection to the innate quality of intuitive knowing emanated from the Self. From this place, the Listener can hear the subtle nuance in the sound and emotions of the Speaker and gain insight. To be able to effectively listen to the Speaker, one must become aware of fear, judgement, and desire to interject or rescue the other person and return their awareness back to loving awareness and deep meditative listening. Through the witness's alignment with their Higher Self, the sharer can borrow strength, bravery, and compassion for their own process, where they may not have been able to access these qualities on their own.

I first read the term "spiritual partnership" in the book *Seat of the Soul* by Gary Zukav. Spiritual Partnership means that we support one another through the stages of life as equals. It means that we hold the highest and best vision of our community members. Each of us has what it takes to hold space for another. All we need is to enjoy deep, conscious breathing and rest in our hearts and allow unconditional love to do the rest.

Holding Space for the World

During this grand transition, we are invited to hold space for the human collective and life on planet Earth as layers of shadow and trauma come to the surface for healing. Many will be in various experiences of distress and chaos. Every moment that we choose to live from our heart, we become a living prayer for a higher destiny outcome for all of the world. We are invited to establish ourselves in Divine Neutrality and be "in The World but not of it." From this middle path, we can participate in the transformation of this planet without getting swept away by sensationalism and polarity. It's OK if you dip into the polarity. When you do, notice what hooks you into the wheel of suffering and do the work to reconcile that part and return to center.

Growing in Compassion

You are not a failure if you cannot hold these qualities for all beings. Therefore, spiritual growth is made of "practices." We use the practices to reclaim our Light. Start simply. Acknowledge the beings and circumstances in your life that are easy to radiate these qualities towards. Notice how it feels to find that illuminated, joyful appreciation towards their beingness and these pleasant living conditions. Then move to someone or something that irritates your inner realm occasionally. Practice transforming the mental attitudes that you hold towards that being or those conditions until you can be rooted firmly in loving-kindness, compassion, empathetic joy, and equanimity.

As you "build it up," you will find confidence and momentum towards your goal of liberation. When you can emulate these qualities towards a person, a group of beings, or some other life conditions that you hold a mild negative charge towards, you can build up towards emulating these qualities towards even the worst of the worst. This does not mean that the other's actions are justified. It just means that you can remove your own judgments and rise above the lower consciousness of victimhood and the conditioned mind. From this place, you become an ambassador of True Peace and a servant towards the liberation of all beings. If someone has harmed you in any way, transform your suffering and pray for their liberation, even to the point of praying they achieve enlightenment faster than you.

As we create more beauty around us and our personal interactions, we hold the space for higher outcomes for us all. We can detach from the mainstream drama and hold space for peace and reconciliation. We can use the power of compassionate listening to become an agent of harmonic transformation in the world. When we hold that prayer and shine with this light, it inspires others. When enough people are aligned with the Source of Light within them, the world will reflect this, and we will create a New Earth.

TWO

Taking Refuge in the Ideal

As spiritual beings on the path of Ascension, we need sources of nourishment to feed our spiritual appetite for Knowledge and Wisdom. Knowledge and Wisdom are the living waters that quench the thirst of the soul. The path of Buddhism describes "The Three Jewels" which I have expanded to encompass an interfaith path.

1. The Enlightened Masters and Ascended Beings (*Buddha*)

There have been souls who have achieved high levels of embodied Truth and Wisdom through their enlightened minds and open hearts in all cultures. Great Masters have incarnated all across the world, and throughout their life, they studied and taught the mysteries of Wisdom and Knowledge. These are the forerunners of consciousness, our spiritual role models. We can look at their examples and emulate the wisdom they embodied.

2. The Teachings of the Masters (*Dharma*)

Sacred texts and enlightened teachings of Oneness and Unconditional Love clearly lay out pathways of remembering the Absolute Reality and the power awakening the limited ego-self to the transcendental infinite Self. Studying the sacred texts helps us to unravel our conditioned mind and reprogram our consciousness to align with Higher Truth.

3. Spiritual Community (*Sangha*)

Spiritual friendships and spiritual partnerships are made of like-minded individuals who empower and support one another on the path of awakening. Everyone is at different stages with their growth. We can glean valuable insight and wisdom gained through experience from our elders, peers, mentors, and teachers. Furthermore, a community that prays together stays together. As we strengthen our bonds through shared spiritual focus, our communities become a liberation force for all beings.

Three Marks of Existence

In Buddhism, there are three pervasive qualities or "marks" of existence: *suffering, impermanence, non-self*. These three marks of existence are a description of inherent qualities of reality and the knower of these principles can use them to transform their reality.

The First Mark of Existence is *dukkha*, suffering. The Buddhists recognize that suffering is inherent in life and that we cannot avoid suffering. Some beings will not incarnate on Earth because of the density of emotional suffering experienced through physical form. You can either get caught up in the illusion and create *karma* here which binds you to the Earth, or you can use suffering for growing into mastery and ascend beyond the need for incarnation. In pre-awakening suffering is seen as a punishment and a prison. In the process of spiritual awakening and high alchemy, suffering is fuel for spiritual transformation and holds the keys to one's liberation when held in the transformative container of loving awareness.

The Second Mark of Existence is *annica*, impermanence. Impermanence means that life is constantly shifting and changing. The whole experience of life and its components and our bodymind complex, our psychophysical self, can be broken into five aggregates or five *skandhas*: material form, sensation, perception, mental formations, and consciousness/awareness that perceives the other *skandhas*.

Each of these components works together to create our mental being. Each of these manifestations has a birth, an existence, and an eventual dissolution. When we become attached to these manifestations, we get swept up in the *maya*, the illusion, and we get lost in *samsara*, the ungraspable world, believing it is real. Remember that spiritual awakening is about learning to discern between what is permanent and what is impermanent, what is real and what is unreal. In the world we live in, the forms, sensations, perceptions, mental formations, and mental awareness are not the true reality. It is but a dream, a temporary appearance, and our task is to awaken and remain conscious while in the dream.

Vairagya, non-attachment, is an inner state where we are disconnected from the pull of the mind, senses, and emotions. First, we can make a mental effort to move the mind away from sensory pleasures. From this place of intentional abstinence, we can see how frequently the mind is drawn towards attaining habitual sensual pleasure (*vyatireka*). From there, we can quiet the senses as we become more aware of the mental attachments and aversions (*ekendriya*). Eventually, this leads us to a neutral state where temptation no longer manifests, and aversion does not exist (*vasirara*).

Para vairagya is a state of supreme detachment, the realization that true happiness comes from within. We are unbound from conditions of the mind and the draw of seeking sensory fulfillment in the world. We can be "in the world but not of it," residing in our Buddha Nature, Christ Nature, Krishna Nature, and our True Self.

Most people spend their lifetimes searching endlessly for the magical component that finally creates a sense of complete fulfillment and lasting happiness. This experience is available for you at this very moment. Take a few moments to breathe long, slow, and deep breaths and release the need to search for something outside of yourself to complete you. Call off the search, even for a moment, and see what is already available for you in fullness.

The Third Mark of Existence is *anatta*, or non-self. When most people think of their "self," they are probably speaking of their physical form, their sensations, their perceptions, their beliefs, or their awareness. Simply, their bodymind complex. All of these have birth, existence, and death so they cannot be the Eternal Self. Even the soul or oversoul are forms and names within the realm of Creation that evolve from one state to another. Our True Self is beyond all names, concepts, and forms. When we look at how the Vedic teachings define *Brahman* as vastness, the Kabbalists speak of *Ain Soph* as Limitless or No-thing, I believe that they are using different perspectives and language to talk of the same thing and each point to the core of our being as this emptiness and vastness.

To understand *annica*, non-self, Buddhism speaks of interbeing, that everything is made up of components of the All. If the sun was not shining, then I could not exist. If rain did not exist, the crops would not exist and therefore, I could not exist. I am part sun. I am part rain. I am a mixture of the All! Everything is interconnected and interrelated, and all components are the by-product of infinite fractals of causality.

To summarize, suffering is inherent in life. We suffer because we cling to the world of form thinking that it is real. We suffer because we forget our True Nature and believe ourselves to be the character we play out in our life. When we accept these three basic concepts, we can begin to unravel our story of suffering and embrace the limitlessness that we truly are!

Three Types of Suffering (Buddhism)

When we begin to awaken, we notice how we have created our own suffering. We begin to detach from stories of victimhood and begin to study the deeper mysteries of our suffering. The Buddhist tradition acknowledges that suffering is inherent in life, and it is up to the seeker to understand the deeper causes of suffering. From the Buddhist perspective, suffering can be separated into three different categories of everyday suffering, the suffering that comes when the conditions of life change, and the background suffering of this world.

One: Everyday Suffering *(dukkha-dukkha)*

There is the inherent suffering of life's difficult moments and stages. This includes physical and mental pain from birth, aging, death, illness, and general distress when life is not going the way we desire.

Two: Suffering of Change *(viparinama-dukkha)*

The suffering that occurs as pleasurable moments and stages shift towards unpleasant experiences. Everything is always changing. Life is impermanent. We suffer when we believe that our experience of the world of names and forms is what brings us joy and wholeness.

Three: Pervasive Suffering *(sankhara-dukkha)*

The suffering that arises from the conditioned mind, the background suffering of existence. This type of suffering arises from unfulfilled desires of the bodymind.

In summary, life inherently has experiences that are not comfortable and cause suffering. "From the womb to the tomb," we all experience dis-ease and discomfort as we go through our life. Life's pleasurable moments will inherently give way to less pleasurable experiences. We suffer when we do not surrender to the changing of time. We suffer because of our uninitiated, conditioned minds. Spiritual knowledge and spiritual practice elevate our minds to become in sync with the perfection of All That Is.

The Four Noble Truths (Buddhism)

The Four Noble Truths of Buddhism are the foundation of the teachings of the Buddha. Understanding the Four Noble Truths helps to liberate one's being from endless cycles of suffering. Simply put, the Four Noble Truths are:

1. Suffering exists.
2. There is a path that leads to suffering.
3. Liberation is possible.
4. There is a pathway that leads to liberation.

1. Truth of Suffering and the Three Marks of Existence

Suffering is inherent in life. 1. From the most subtle discomfort to the most extreme and excruciating pain, life contains a full spectrum of experiences that cause suffering. 2. Impermanence (*anicca*) is inherent in life. Life circumstances are always shifting and changing. It is our attachments to the world of form that causes suffering. 3. We also suffer because there is suffering in the world and our conditioned mind creates suffering because of ignorance. Grasping at and chasing after sensory experiences eventually brings us to the truth that true fulfillment comes from internal, spiritual growth.

2. Truth of the Cause of Suffering

The cause and origin of suffering, *samudaya*, is attachment, craving, and desire. When we chase sensory experiences for their temporary fulfillment, we suffer. When we desire to be something other than who we are in the present moment, we put ourselves in a prison of suffering. When we try to stop life experiences from happening, our fear and resistance create suffering. The three poisons of greed, hatred, and ignorance limit our light and keep us in cycles of suffering.

When we believe something outside of our self will complete us, we believe in the illusion, and we endlessly search outside of ourselves for the magical component that will end our suffering. Our senses drag us through our lives as if we are being pulled by wild horses in every direction. Therefore, many wisdom traditions value sensory deprivation (*pratyahara* in Sanskrit). When we retract our senses and turn inward, we detach from the eternal shifting of the physical universe and begin to empty ourselves of all the thoughts that create suffering so that we can discover the treasure that lives within our very being.

3. Truth of the End of Suffering

Redemption is available for all souls who wish to awaken. If we want to end our suffering, we can continuously acknowledge our power to awaken to higher consciousness. As we release the misperception that happiness and wholeness are found outside of us, we begin to discover the keys to our liberation found within our own being. As we hold to the truth that liberation is possible, we begin to discern what is resonant with our higher path and what is not. We begin to detach ourselves from the Wheel of Karma (*samsara*) and the endless cycle of reincarnation and death.

It should be reiterated that "stepping off the wheel" of endless reincarnations is the birthright for those who choose to follow the path of Ascension all the way through in this life. It may be hard for some to envision this world without suffering of any kind. It may even seem impossible. Yet, for those who are willing to completely release all of their misidentifications and misperceptions, full liberation is theirs to claim, and it shall be theirs!

4. Truth of the Path that Leads to the End of Suffering

The Buddhist's path of liberating one's consciousness from suffering is through "Right Understanding." Right understanding is knowing that there is no fixed self (*anatta*), suffering is inherent in life (*dukkha*), and life's conditions are impermanent (*anicca*). The sacred scriptures of India, Tibet, Egypt, and the mystic traditions like the Gnostics and Kabbalists contain detailed instructions for freeing one's consciousness from the mind's conditioning. There are as many paths to salvation as there are humans upon the planet. There is no "one path fits all" formula. The one principle found at the core of all the wisdom traditions is the redemptive power of unconditional love.

In the teachings of Vedanta, they say, "The knower of Brahman attains the highest." Meaning that nothing of this illusory world will give you the richness that God-realization can give you. You could add up all the riches of the universe and it will still not add up to the immense treasure that is your divine inheritance. The ingathering of spiritual Light is attained through ritualized connection with Source, with the Absolute, through routine spiritual practices aiming to dissolve the negative influences of the ego and merge consciously with the Oneness of All That Is. This leads us to true liberation from cycles of suffering. Practice! Practice! Practice! Source-realization can be yours!

THREE

Path of Nondual Knowledge

Patanjali's *Yoga Sutras*, a treatise on classical yoga, describes eight limbs of the yogic practices that aid the practitioner on their path of awakening and God-Self Realization. This path was expanded on in the work of the great Indian philosopher Shankaracharya such as in the text *Aparokshanabhuti.* In this text he describes his fifteen-fold path which merges *raja yoga*, the path of meditation, *with jnana yoga*, the path of knowledge, using the non-dual teachings of *Advaita Vedanta*. Pitanjali's eight limbs are noted with *.

Central to Advaita Vedanta is the concept that only Brahman, the Divine Consciousness is real and that all of Creation and its many manifestations arise, exist, and dissolve within that One Consciousness. That Atman, the inner Source Consciousness, our true Self, is seen as the same as Brahman. We are that One Light of Consciousness, and we only perceive ourselves as separate limited beings with a bodymind stuck in cycles of suffering and reincarnation because we have forgotten our True Nature as the pure Light of Source.

The fifteen-fold path is summarized as follows:

1. *Yama* (ethical observances for all is Source/Self) *
2. *Niyama* (self-conduct for all is Source/Self) *
3. *Tyaga* (*renunciation of the world, fullness comes from Source/Self*)
4. *Mauna* (*silence for revealing Source/Self*)
5. *Desha* (*auspicious place, no distractions from Source/Self*)
6. *Kala* (*auspicious time, Source/Self is now.*)
7. *Asana* (comfortable posture to think about Source/Self) *
8. *Mulabandha* (*restraining root lock, rooting awareness in Source/Self.*)
9. *Dehasmya* (*straightening body, merging body with Source/Self*)
10. *Druk Stiti* (*fixing of the gaze to see Source/Self everywhere*)
11. *Pranayama* (control pranic force by maintaining Source/Self connection) *
12. *Pratyahara* (sense withdrawal, withdrawal of the mind from sense experiences, immersing the mind in Source) *

13. *Dharana* (concentration, focus on the object of meditation, keeping mind on Source/Self) *
14. *Dhyana* (single-pointed focus/meditation on Source/Self) *
15. *Samadhi* (absorption into Oneness of Source/Self) *

ONE: The Yamas

The Yamas are a set of inner observances, restraints (the "don'ts") and universal ethics that lead towards the balance of Life. From the knowing that all is Source and Source is your True Self from a non-dual perspective, we can use the Yamas to control the senses to bring about non-dual focus and Self-realization.

Ahimsa: Non-harming, Non-violence

Kindness and compassion are the core of spiritual growth and the root of all spiritual virtues. All beings have the right to life, liberty, and the pursuit of higher consciousness. Practicing *ahimsa* soothes old suffering and keeps us from creating more suffering in the world.

Satya: Benevolent Truthfulness

Benevolent truthfulness means that we do not speak falsely and mislead others. When sharing truth, we do it gently. It also means that we do not divulge information when we know that it will harm someone. Practicing *satya* exercises your right to dignity. People learn that they can rely on you to be honest and dependable when sharing your truth.

Asteya: Non-stealing

Non-stealing means not taking anything that is not rightfully yours. Everyone has the right to property, yet we should live within balance. Renunciation of materialistic conditioning and sharing from a generous heart are expressions of *asteya*.

Brahmacharya: Right use of Energy, Sexual Harmony

This observance means that we use our life force energy towards the freedom of suffering of ourselves and all beings. This includes using our sexual life force in a way that honors the divinity and heart of another.

Aparigraha: Non-greed or Non-hoarding

Greed and hoarding stem from separation consciousness and the belief that we will not have enough of what we need to survive. *Aparigraha* is rooted in the belief that we are always being provided with what we need to sustain our path.

Refrain from intoxication (Buddhism)

Mindfulness and responsibility, the ability to respond with maturity and compassion, grow when the mind and senses are not dulled and degraded by adulterants and powerful sensory experiences. Abstaining from addictive patterns and intoxication helps us remain clear and heart-centered so that we can make appropriate observations and compassionate actions.

TWO: The Niyamas

The *Niyamas* are a set of observances in self-conduct (the "do's") that increase a sense of commonality and a sense of oneness, harmony, and bliss that leads towards knowledge of one's True Nature and Higher Self.

Saucha: Cleanliness

Purifying the mind, body, and spirit with spiritual practices and higher wisdom harmonizes our thoughts, intentions, actions, and habits. This means not only taking care of our inner realm but also tending to our physical experience and the environment we inhabit.

Santosha: Contentment

Growing in acceptance and gratitude for current life circumstances, creating a sense of optimism. Even if life is challenging, we can appreciate what we have and the opportunity to grow.

Tapas: Discipline, Austerity, Burning Enthusiasm

Honoring the inner fire that drives us to evolve and do what is noble and good for our path. This often means going against the grain of our deeply imprinted patterns and beliefs. Discipline in our pursuit of true liberation is the fire that burns away our karma, moving us out of cycles of repeated suffering and into higher states of freedom.

Svadhyaya: **Study of Self and Sacred Texts**

To truly "know thyself," we practice reflection and self-inquiry. We source wisdom through the examples of the enlightened masters, the knowledge from sacred texts, and use our spiritual community as sacred mirrors, reflecting back to us our current state of consciousness.

Isvara Pranidhana: **Surrender to Supreme Contemplation of the Higher Power**

We express this quality when we dedicate our lives to the Service of All. We continuously surrender our will to the Divine Will of Source and the Higher Evolution. Our life becomes a moving prayer, an act of reverence for and devotion towards the Love of the Universe.

THREE: Tyaga (renunciation)

In this observance, we are constantly disengaging our mind from the pull of the world, identification with the bodymind, and the illusion that true happiness comes from any finite experience. As we renounce those notions we can source our wholeness from the Source within us, our true Self. From here we can dissolve our inner distortions and see the divinity within all of Creation while also recognizing that all of our experiences are arising within the consciousness of the Self. In this awareness we understand that the material reality and our possessions are not what bring us lasting fulfillment. Practicing minimizing our material possessions is an expression of this observance.

FOUR: Mauna (silence)

Ultimate reality is beyond speech and language so we must find inner silence and outer silence to meditate on the Self and the divine deeply. Many spiritual traditions have practices of verbal silence and quiet isolation so that one can focus on the deepest Self and divine consciousness reality. Having one day a week of silence and contemplation is a powerful practice with many benefits. Practicing silence in community can reveal a lot about the dynamics of how we relate to one another.

FIVE: Desha (auspicious place)

Our spiritual practice (*sadhana*) is amplified in potency when we are in an environment conducive to focus, having as little distractions as possible. Our personal practice is best done in solitude within a harmonic space to train the mind to expand into the all-pervasive space of the Divine found within and without. Practicing in the same space repeatedly creates a positive field that supports and regenerates the practitioner with each continuous session.

SIX: Kala (auspicious time)

Our personal practice is amplified in potency when we align the timing of our practice with natural rhythms and auspicious astrological events such as sunrises, sunsets, new and full moons, equinoxes and solstices and other auspicious times. Doing your practice at the same time each day is another way of working with this observation. Ultimately, training the mind to be established in the eternal unfolding of the now moment, trains us to use each sacred moment as a time of spiritual practice. Source is right here, right now.

SEVEN: Asana (posture)

Many are familiar with the *hatha yoga* postures known in Sanskrit as *asanas*. As one settles into a posture, one moves the center of one's consciousness deeper and deeper to the vantage point of pure non-dual awareness, from the comfortable seat of pure awareness. This helps to train the mind to continuously focus on the Supreme Reality, the Kingdom of God that exists within us and all around us.

EIGHT: Mulabandha (restraining root lock)

In meditation and asana practice, one is guided to use the root lock, a lifting of the pelvic floor, to stabilize the physical body, focus the mind, and direct pranic force up through pranic tube along the spinal column. With intention, the dedicated practitioner uses this practice to establish their consciousness on the Divine, the root of one's existence, with increasing consistency.

NINE: Dehasmya (straightening the body)

Conscious embodiment practices train the entirety of the body and mind to work with alignment, precision, and symbiotic harmony. Similarly, we can train the entirety of our bodymind complex to work in symbiosis with the Divine as we practice merging our consciousness with the higher consciousness reality. In this way we walk straight on our path of righteousness and nobility as conscious embodiments of divine will in action.

TEN: Druk Stiti (fixing the gaze)

This speaks to not only how one holds one's gaze during meditation practice but also how we train awareness to see the divine in all. While our physical eyes look upon this world, our inner eye of knowledge can be focused on the divine consciousness reality.

ELEVEN: Pranayama (control of pranic force)

In many traditions there are practices of breathing to increase life force and purify the bodymind. One can elevate the practice by using the four stages of the breath to focus on the Source of Eternal Life and shed attachment to the material universe. An example of this is:

Breathing in: I am Divine Consciousness (*aham brahmasmi*)

Exhalation: releasing attachment to external reality and thought

TWELVE: Pratyahara (withdrawal of the senses)

In some yogic practices, one may limit sensory experiences such as by covering the eyes or ears to assist with inward focus of the mind towards the divine Self. When moving about one's life, a dedicated practitioner uses all experiences to see the Self, the divine consciousness, operating in the background of all experiences.

THIRTEEN: Dharana (focus on the object of meditation)

In meditative practices, a focus point is used to steady the fluctuations of the mind. Beyond typical concentration and holding the gaze on a particular physical location, one can train the activities of the mind to focus on the Divine Reality wherever the mind journeys.

FOURTEEN: Dhyana (meditation)

Various practices of meditation are found throughout the many wisdom traditions of the Earth. The highest intention and practice of meditation is *Atma Dhyana*, meditation on the Supreme Self. As we train the mind to continuously focus on the divine reality, within and without, we establish and stabilize our mental activity on the truth that we are that infinite existence consciousness bliss. The essence and power of this high spiritual truth is felt and declared in the mantras of *aham brahmasmi*, I am Brahman, or I am that I AM.

FIFTEEN: Samadhi (Oneness)

Spiritual practice transforms our mind from a carnal, animalistic nature to that of divine consciousness. In the initial stages of awakening, we experience dullness, agitation, breaks in attention, attachments to sensory experiences, suffering, distraction, attachment to bliss, and even blankness of mind. When one is able to continuously maintain the awareness that "I am Divine Consciousness" one is absorbed into the reality of the highest truth, the supreme reality of existence consciousness bliss resulting in the state that goes by many names in many traditions including *samadhi, nirvana,* and salvation.

FOUR

Spiritual Ethics

The Eightfold Path of Buddhism offers us a set of ethical observances to help us grow in nobility. The practice of these observances is an ongoing reflection fueled by personal revelations. They help us to live a peaceful and orderly existence in the community. Practicing these values and virtues keeps us from creating more negative karma or from adding to the suffering of the world. These values meet the practitioner where they are on their path of awakening. Every life experience is valuable as we learn to discern what is essential for life and what distracts us from and distorts our vision of our True Nature.

The Eightfold Path of Buddhism is a guide to spiritual awakening and liberation from cycles of suffering. This path consists of moral conduct, mental discipline, and the attainment of divine wisdom. The word "*samma*," a Pali word, is often translated as "right." When used in this context, right is not describing a system of "right" and "wrong," but quality of expression rooted in compassion and illuminated by Higher Wisdom. As we learn to walk the path of righteous nobility guided by a loving heart, we embody the potential of the liberation of all beings from the cycles of suffering.

The root quality of these morals is *ahimsa*, nonviolence, and non-harming. We can look at our life or our consciousness as a garden. In our garden, we have many varieties of seeds planted. Some seeds are seeds of suffering. Some of these seeds are of compassion and love. In every moment, we have a choice to water our seeds of suffering or water our seeds of love and compassion. Living a righteous and noble life is a practice of watering the seeds of compassion and love. Make your garden beautiful by watering seeds of patience, tenderness, kindness, gentleness, and other qualities of love and compassion.

One: Right Understanding, Right View (Samma Ditthi)

The Four Noble Truths and the Three Characteristics of Existence can help us to better understand the nature of reality. We understand that how we see our self is always shifting and changing and that life is impermanent. We understand that suffering is inherent in life and that pleasurable moments eventually shift to less pleasurable moments. We understand we suffer because we hold conditioning from this world. We understand that not only does suffering occur but there is also a path to suffering. We understand liberation is possible and that there is a pathway to liberation.

Two: Right Intent, Right Resolve (Samma Sankappa)

This is our commitment to the path of awakening and dedication towards the liberation of all beings from suffering. This happens by guiding one's thoughts and intentions back to Unconditional Love and Oneness and dedicating our beingness to Service to All.

Three: Right Speech (Samma Vaca)

We can use our communication to relieve suffering and create harmonic agreements. This includes refraining from lying, using divisive or abusive speech, slander, and even idle gossip. Often people use communication to distract themselves from fully experiencing their Inner Being. Gandhi said, "Speak only if it improves upon the silence." Before communicating, ask yourself, "Is it kind? Is it true? Is it necessary? Is it helpful?"

Four: Right Action (Samma Kammanta)

With right action, we dedicate all actions of the body towards compassionate living and to relieving the suffering of all sentient beings. This includes nonviolence, non-stealing, and sacred sexuality.

Five: Right Livelihood (Samma Ajiva)

Our livelihood, our way of generating income, gathering resources, and creating a career path should be done honestly and in a way that promotes equality among all sentient life. This means that our work does not harm other beings or nature and that our participation in society reflects our Service to the Greater Good of Life.

Six: Right Effort (Samma Vayama)

We strive to train the mind towards wholesome, positive thoughts that create positive, life-affirming action. We grow in an "attitude of gratitude," shedding negative thoughts and making a conscious effort to move towards joyful determination.

Seven: Right Mindfulness (Samma Sati)

We practice training the mind and our conscious awareness to be fully focused on the present moment. This includes growing in our awareness of the body, feelings, mind, thoughts, breath, and the ever-shifting phenomenon that we call reality.

Eight: Right Concentration (Samma Samadhi)

This is the practice of joining the mind with the Absolute. Seeing Heaven on Earth through single-pointed meditation, which results in unbroken attentiveness and a deep feeling of tranquility and bliss.

Creating Pathways of Transformation

While each of us has different karma, different mental patterning, and different soul contracts, there are simple key principles that can be applied to any negative condition to transform it into a higher state. If we wish to purify our bodymind complex, we need to follow fours steps:

1. Cease to deny the presence of patterns within our mind that cause suffering for ourselves and others.
2. Cease justification of those patterns.
3. Release guilt around the patterns of distortion and limitation that we carry.
4. Actively seek out and practice methods of purification and God/Self-realization.

Mental Alchemy: Evolving to Higher Thought

The mind is constantly generating thoughts. Some are pleasant and empowering, and others are generated from the shadows of our unprocessed trauma and ignorance. When one becomes aware of negative thoughts that keep us in cycles of suffering, we have three options to make change.

1. Discard the thought, jerk it out of the mind.
2. Discard the thought for a higher vibrational thought. ("I bind this thought pattern of anger. I call forth and set loose the power of serenity.)
3. Intensify the thought/emotion and direct it towards Source such as in the tantric traditions. This option should be done with caution as intensifying powerful negative emotion/desire/thought can cause more chaos and suffering.

Seven Pillars of Personal Transformation)

Below are seven keys for personal transformation to guide you through your awakening and ascension processes. Use each key to fine-tune your actions to create lasting positive change.

One: Sankalpa — Intention

Intention is everything on the path of awakening. *Sankalpa* is an intention that comes from the heart and serves your Higher Path. Sometimes we have unconscious intentions of avoiding suffering or discomfort, which keep us from going through the experiences that give valuable insight into the nature of our suffering. This concept is reflected in Newton's First Law of Motion which states that an object will remain at rest or motion until acted upon by another force. Your intention is the force that creates the architecture and trajectory of your future.

Attention and *intention* are qualities of consciousness. *Attention* energizes consciousness. Wherever the mind goes, the energy follows, and we become increasingly aware of what we focus upon. *Intention* transforms whatever we hold within the container of our awareness.

Intention shapes our destiny. Unconscious intentions are those of our subconscious and often operate in the background. Most of humanity operates with the unconscious intention to survive and protect their body and future. They haphazardly fumble through life from one event to another, from one emotional reaction to another, asleep in their own dream.

As we awaken and begin to become deliberate conscious creators of our reality, we begin to focus our intention and attention in a way that sustains us on our path of spiritual growth and personal mastery.

Two: Tapas — Intensity and Dedication

This is related to Newton's Second Law of Motion, which states, "The rate of change of momentum of a body with respect to time is directly proportional to the net external force acting on the body." Spiritual growth is dependent on the intensity and duration of our practice. Our commitment can be seen as low, medium, or high intensity.

Three: Shani — Slowing

Becoming aware of our subconscious drives requires us to slow down our physical, mental, and emotional actions to understand the subtle and nuanced shifts in our consciousness. While high-intensity practices may result in faster spiritual growth, it is important to discern when rest and a gentler pace are what is most needed.

Four: Vidya — Deep Awareness, Clear Sight

Self-inquiry and mindfulness help us see and understand our habits and self-limiting, self-sabotaging patterns to transform them into higher states. Mindfulness of any condition immediately begins to transform the condition into a higher state through loving awareness.

Five: Abhaya — Fearlessness, Bravery

Change takes courage. Lasting change requires us to acknowledge our fear but not let it dictate our actions or inaction. Pushing our edge requires us to be comfortable within the discomfort and release our need for external validation, anchoring us to our own internal compass of truth.

Six: Darshana — Inspired Vision

Having a vision of what the higher outcome looks and feels like is essential to our path of spiritual growth. When we want to create new patterns, we can create an inner image of our ideal life when we are free of the limiting patterns and beliefs of the ego and subconscious patterns.

Seven: Abhyasa — Persistent Practice

Spiritual growth is not linear. It winds, curves, backslides, and stagnates at times. There are no "failures" or wrong ways on the spiritual path. There are only opportunities to reflect, gain insight, and practice again.

Moving Beyond Limitation

To create lasting change, one needs to cultivate *discipline*, an attitude and actions that are of *service* to others, and consistent *practice* towards one's higher goals. *Discipline* is the fire that drives and is needed to build momentum in a new direction. *Service* to others helps us step out of the limitations of the false ego and into universal connection. Through spiritual *practice*, the unconscious becomes conscious, and we can choose to step out of the patterns that cause suffering in our lives and move into higher states of freedom. It is said that over ninety percent of our cognitive processes are subconscious, operating mostly in the background undetected. Deeply ingrained unconscious beliefs are like ghosts that haunt our consciousness, driving us towards frustration and limiting patterns. Spiritual growth is dependent on awareness and action taken in a positive direction to mature our consciousness and heal the echoes of past trauma that call out from our subconscious and unconscious minds.

Growth takes time and comes in stages. We can look at the progression of the evolution of personal transformation in four stages:

1. **Unconsciously Incompetent:** Before we become aware of limiting beliefs and self-destructive patterns, we are unaware that we lack the skills needed to move out of cycles of suffering.
2. **Consciously Incompetent:** When the pattern is revealed through the light of our awareness, we become aware of the pattern and our

lack of the skills and knowledge required to move into a higher state of living. At this stage, we can seek information and guidance to lead us onto a higher path and a higher perspective. We likely cycle back through the old patterns as we refine our intentions and actions and gather more data to support our new path. Compassion, forgiveness, and grace help us understand that we are not our past behaviors, and we are on a path of learning and discovery.

3. **Consciously Competent:** Once we start to implement our newfound insights, we move out of a pattern of limitation and into a higher state. There is still an awareness of the impulses and momentum of our old habits, but the persistent practice has laid a new path for us to journey on and we become increasingly more confident on our new trajectory.

4. **Unconsciously Competent:** After consistent practice, we fully integrate the new way of being and become completely rooted in our new path. Since we have transformed our subconscious beliefs through spiritual practice, the old ways fade completely into the past and we enjoy our new way of being.

Now you should have a foundational understanding of spirituality, spiritual awakening, and the path out of suffering and bondage. Now we will explore how to apply the practices of spiritual alchemy to catalyze multidimensional awakening and true liberation. Set your intentions and diligently dedicate yourself to your path. Slow yourself down and deepen your awareness. Face the challenges of life with bravery while keeping your inner focus on your inspired vision of Heaven on Earth. There is much love and support for you. Practice! Practice! Practice! All is coming!

FIVE

Meditation

The main tool for spiritual alchemy is the practice of concentration and meditation. Meditation is the experience of single-pointed focus which occurs through practices of mindfulness and concentration. There are countless benefits of practicing meditation including stress relief, liberation from fear of death, development of magnetism in your personality, reduction of heart rate and blood pressure, reduction of inflammation, lowering of cortisol in the body, and elevating spiritual connection. Simply put, meditation helps us create the conditions for the mind to be as useful as possible. When the mind is calm, it translates into the other layers of our being.

In modern society, it is common knowledge that meditation is an excellent tool for personal transformation. The challenge for individuals is twofold. One issue is developing confidence and skill. The other is dedication and commitment to do the practice. My suggestion for those new to meditation is to find a teacher to walk you through the basics of meditation so that you do not get discouraged in the early stages. Then commit to doing the practices for at least 10-20 minutes a day. New Earth Ascending has instructional videos to get you started!

Many different types of meditation exist. Some are passive practices like seated or supine (laying on the back) meditation practices. Some are active movement practices that develop mindful awareness like hatha yoga and qi gong. Try a variety of practices until you find one that feels right and then repeatedly perform that method to unlock its benefits. I highly recommend finding an experienced guide to instruct you with new meditation techniques so that you can quickly develop confidence and skill in the art of meditation. If you find that you have a hard time quieting the mind, combine active practices to regulate and focus the bodymind and then move into stillness practices to go deeper within.

Meditation practices most often involve conscious breathing to unite the physical body and subtle bodies in your awareness. Tuning in to the breath at the beginning of meditation practice is like saddling up on a horse for a journey. Focusing on the breath trains the mind for the journey inward and helps to regulate the autonomic nervous system so that you are relaxed and calm but focused and alert for the journey.

As we progress in meditation practice and throughout our day, we move through five stages of the mind:

1. *Mudham*: dull, forgetful, delusion, and lethargic.
2. *Kshiptam*: raving, wandering, restless, distracted, disturbed state of mind.
3. *Vikshiptam*: oscillating, occasionally steady, easily distracted, thought in process of purification.
4. *Ekaagram*: one-pointed, tranquil, focused, concentrated.
5. *Niruddham*: restrained, cessation of the waves of the mind, controlled, regulated, highly mastered.

Many people give up on meditation because they erroneously believe that they should be able to immediately quiet the mind. When beginning to work with meditative practices, it is expected that a person will naturally be in stages one and two as one develops the awareness and skill needed to move into quieter, more focused states of the mind. Awareness is the first step to creating positive change. The process of developing meditative skill is accelerated when guided by an experienced teacher or when meditating with others. Drop all expectations of what meditation is supposed to look like or feel like and keep practicing stillness and awareness. All is coming!

Meditation Guidelines

Posture

Some practices ask that you are seated with your spine erect. This is not always easy and comfortable for people. I suggest using pillows and blankets to prop yourself into a comfortable position, sitting in a chair, sitting with your back against a wall, or laying down flat if seated positioning is not easy for you. What is important is that the spine is long and that you are comfortable. Seated meditation practice allows the spine to act as an antennae system with the Earth and has many benefits such as strengthening or elongating certain muscle groups, and you are less likely to fall asleep in a seated meditation posture.

Breathe through the Nose

Most breathing practices focus on nasal breathing. Breathing through the nose filters and adjusts the temperature of the air to prepare it to pass through the body. Breathing through the mouth releases life force energy through the moisture that is exhaled in the breath. If you are congested or inhibited in any way, it is perfectly fine to breathe through the mouth.

Diaphragmatic Breathing

The diaphragm is our bridge between the higher spiritual chakras and our lower earthly chakras. When we breathe primarily from our chest, we are ungrounded and floating off the ground. When we focus on initiating breath with the diaphragm and allow the lower abdomen to expand and contract with each breath, this creates a sense of being grounded and connected to the Earth. It also massages our internal organs. To get the most from our breath, we should use "yogic breathing" or three-part breathing to use the full range of movement of breath in the lungs. This is explained more in the *pranamaya kosha* section.

Focus the Mind

Notice all four stages of the breath, including inhalation, retention, exhalation, and suspension. Equalize and extend each stage to create an effortless rhythm. If the mind wanders, bring it back to feeling the sensations of breathing. You can also use affirmations and counting to keep the mind focused on the experience of breathing.

Watching the Breath

The foundation of meditation practice is breath awareness. It is like the horse that you saddle onto for the journey of meditation. As you breathe in and out, deepen your awareness on the experience of breathing. This alone can create powerful energy and clarity. You can use numbers to train the mind into the present moment. For example, breathing in for a count of four, holding for four, exhaling for four, and pausing for four. This trains the mind to be solely focused on the act of breathing. Using a mental mantra or affirmation helps to train the thought patterns to focus on the intention of the meditation. For example, as you breathe in, focus fully on all the sensations of breathing in and mentally say to yourself, "I am aware that I am breathing in." As you exhale, focus fully on all the qualities of breathing out and say to yourself, "I am aware that I am breathing out." This can be simplified to "breathing in" and "breathing out." This practice is my first recommendation for new meditators.

Be Gentle on Yourself

If breathwork or meditative practices add stress to the body or mind, stop immediately, and return to normal breathing. Breathing patterns can be difficult to break. No one is expecting you to master this right away. When you are calm, you can try again.

Emotional Release

It is not uncommon for people to experience a myriad of thoughts, sensations, and emotions as they begin to practice conscious breathing and meditation. Sometimes, powerful emotions can surface that are remnants of unprocessed trauma and past experiences. If this happens, continue to breathe deep and calm breaths and allow the emotional energy to be felt and released.

Energy Movement and Sensations

When we breathe consciously and deeply, we oxygenate the blood and tissues much more than they are used to. This can create tingling sensations, involuntary muscle contractions, heat, and other sensations. Stay calm and continue breathing slowly and deeply to continue moving the energy. If it startles you too much, you can slow down or take a rest.

Basic Meditation Procedure

1. Find a comfortable seated position.
2. Adjust your posture to ensure that you can sit easily for a while with a long, vertical spine. Use props like a wall, meditation pillow, blankets, or a chair to support the body's positioning.
3. Aim for body stillness (*kaya sthairyam*) and progressive relaxation. (Scan the body to soften tension and align the bone structure.)
4. Practice breath awareness (*anapanasati*).
5. Observe the inner planes from a place of witnessing and non-attachment.

6. Add additional practices like *mantra*, breathwork, and visualization to enhance the practice.
7. Experience thoughtless state (move in and out of 6 and 7).
8. Return to waking state of consciousness.

Various Methods of Meditation

Mindfulness Meditation

One type of meditation is mindfulness/witnessing practices. All meditation methods have this quality of paying attention to what arises in one's experience with increasing mental awareness of subtlety and nuance. Mindfulness can be cultivated while breathing, walking, dancing, talking, yoga asana, tai chi, or any other normal day-to-day activities like riding a bike or washing dishes. Every moment holds an opportunity to cultivate mindfulness.

Sublime State Meditation

There is a lot of benefit in simply meditating on the sublime states or virtues such as Peace, Equanimity, Kindness, Compassion, and Joy. Simply evoke the state and supporting imagery in your mind and breathe into it as you allow yourself to bask in the Love and Light of the Sublime.

Antar Mouna: Inner Silence

This meditative practice was made famous by Swami Satyananda, and I discovered additional steps in an article written by yoga teacher trainer Christian Möllenhoff. "*Antar*" means inner and "*mouna*" means stillness. This practice helps you understand the complex functions of the mind so that you can develop a tranquil state of inner silence. The stages of the practice are as follows:

1. Setting up body sturdiness (posture and breath awareness).
2. Externalizing awareness of the senses.
3. Awareness of spontaneous thought processes.
4. Creating thought sequences and willfully stopping them.
5. Awareness and discarding spontaneous thoughts.
6. Awareness of Inner Space (chidakasha) and Emptiness.
7. Alternating between Step 2 and Step 6.
8. Resting in Universal Beingness, Atman.

Mantra Meditation

Another type of meditation is mantra meditation. A person recites, out loud or internally, repetitive thoughts or spoken words that bring the practitioner into loving awareness, unity, and personal empowerment. Many traditions use mantras to create alchemical changes in consciousness, especially in the Tibetan, Vedic, and Jewish traditions. The use of the holy names of the Divine and holy mantras connects the practitioner with the momentum of all the other practitioners who have used these same vibrations throughout all of time and space, including the higher dimensions. These mantras focus the practitioner on higher thoughtforms outside of the mind's conditioning and begin a process of transmutation that happens on all levels of one's being including the DNA. Mantra meditations are also preventative medicine for the consciousness as they protect the mind from absorbing lower thoughtforms.

Mantras or devotional songs in your native language that come from the heart are often the most powerful. If you have any hesitation about reciting mantras in another language, stick with your own language. Here are some mantras from non-English traditions that I have learned that have been helpful in my own healing and transformation. I recommend learning a variety of mantras and devotional songs to infuse many varieties of higher consciousness thoughtforms into your system.

Om/Aum (Sanskrit)

Translates as the primordial sound of Creation, the sound that began all vibrations in Creation. Reciting OM opens the body-mind-Source connection and works at bringing all systems into the original harmonic resonance. Chanting OM alchemically leads us through the four states of consciousness of waking, dreaming, deep sleep, and supreme equilibrium within the sounds of A-U-M and the silence that follows.

Gate Gate Para Gate Parasam Gate Bodhi Svaha (Sanskrit)

"Going, going, going on beyond, always going on beyond, always becoming enlightened"

This mantra connects us to the Higher Evolution of consciousness, moving us from what is currently known and experienced in limitation towards our own Buddhahood and liberated mastery. An extra layer of intention is that recitation of this mantra not only supports your ascension but also extends to assist the ascension of all of life.

Kadoish Kadoish Kadoish Adonai Tsabayoth (Hebrew)

"Holy! Holy! Holy! Lord God of Hosts"

This mantra connects us to the many higher consciousness light beings that serve the Living Light, activating multidimensional transformation for the practitioner.

Lokah Samastah Sukhino Bhavantu (Sanskrit)

"May all beings be free of suffering. May all my words, thoughts, and actions contribute towards that liberation." or *"May all beings be filled with joy, love, and light!"*

Mindful Breathing with Mental Mantra (Ajapa Japa)

Another way to practice is to shift from verbal mantra recitation to mental recitation. Start with a few rounds of your favorite mantra articulating each sound and feeling the meaning and wisdom of the mantra. Then silently repeat the mantra to yourself in your mind while also feeling the meaning and wisdom shining throughout your inner being. In this way, the mantra continues to play in the subconscious throughout the day to elevate the brain patterning.

Trataka Meditation

Another type of meditation is Trataka meditation, which includes focusing one's mind on a single object to induce a trance and inner focus. This is commonly done with a candle, sun gazing, and *yantras* (sacred geometric designs with psychic healing effects). As the practitioner concentrates on the object, they simultaneously remain unattached to any intruding thoughts to develop a state of clarity. Trataka can also be done by imagining that the sacred images or symbols are superimposed on the screen of the mind or in the heart field to bring the qualities of the object of meditation into the inner realm.

When working with a candle, be sure the flame is at eye level, motionless, and that the room is as dark as possible. Stare into the candle while holding meditative awareness. Resist the urge to blink for as long as possible while holding single-pointed focus on the flame. Allow the tears to emerge. When you can no longer hold the gaze, close the eyes and allow the tears to wash through the eyes while holding an inner image of the candle flame. When the image fades, you can begin another round of Trataka. Additionally, you may add mental mantra recitation.

Focusing on an object for even less than a minute cultivates a relaxed mind and a relaxed body. This is commonly experienced in "road hypnosis" when someone loses a chunk of time while driving because of their mind's focus on the road. This also happens when someone is listening to another person speak. We have about twenty to thirty seconds to make a point when we are communicating with others before they start to slip into a hypnotic trance.

I suggest practicing mindfulness if you are watching a TV screen or scrolling through smart devices as these technologies quickly move us into a hypnotic trance with a high level of suggestibility where other thoughts and attitudes can be implanted into our subconscious. When we use these technologies with mindfulness, we know when content is not good for our mind, and we can avoid being programmed subconsciously by changing the content or turning off the device.

Guided Visualization Meditation

Another type of meditation is guided visualization or imaginative meditation using the inner technology of the *chidakasha,* the screen of the mind. In guided visualization, the practitioner visualizes imagery through their imagination to evoke certain emotional experiences such as imagining peaceful scenery like flowing water or sunny fields of flowers to evoke a sense of peace and tranquility. Practitioners can imagine light formations to raise their vibration, like being within a bubble of white light. This practice can be expanded into advanced psychic practices like remote viewing and astral projection as the practitioner learns to project their nonlocal consciousness to other places and times. We do this every night when we sleep as our astral body travels to learn and heal in other realms.

Yoga Nidra

Yoga Nidra is a practice of "yogic sleep" where the practitioner is led through waking consciousness into a deep relaxation that mimics the experience of deep sleep and then intentionally guided back into waking consciousness. This is a great practice to do if you have trouble sleeping or need to take a quick yogic nap to rejuvenate yourself during the day. It is best to have this pre-recorded or have someone lead you through the stages of the process.

Repeated Practice Leads to Mastery

Find a practice or two that you feel resonant with and practice it every day to get used to it. The longer and more consistently you practice, the more benefit and mastery you will experience. After you understand the basics of these practices, you will likely find yourself using them throughout your day. It is perfectly normal to be challenged at first or to have practice sessions that are more challenging with the "monkey mind" jumping from thought to thought. Compassionately accept where you are in your process and keep practicing!

SIX

Koshas: Layers of Being

The human body is a multilayered system of subtle energy fields of various vibrational frequencies that are in a constant state of transformation. What people typically call their "body" is actually several different bodies overlapping one another. *Kosha* is a Sanskrit word for "sheaths" as it describes the different bodies fitting into one another like a sword into its scabbard. Each one fits inside the other like Russian nesting dolls or a hand fitting into a glove. Each layer is inserted into, pervades, and extends beyond the previous. Each exists in its own bandwidth, its own density, from the most physical to the ultradimensional part of us that exists beyond this illusory world. We are truly multidimensional holographic beings of Light!

The term 'holarchy' is a word created by fusing together 'whole' and 'hierarchy' to describe individual components which have their own wholeness but contribute to a greater wholeness and unification. The human body is a mirror reflection of the greater cosmological order. Just as Source is the greater sphere which all other spheres of creation exist within, the Source within us lays the foundation for the other layers of our being to emerge.

While each layer is whole and has its own functions and properties, each layer contributes to the greater wholeness of our being. We separate each layer to understand its components, functions, and purpose, yet we should keep in mind that each layer contributes to the entire hologram of our being and all layers interpenetrate, occupy the same space, and work in symbiotic relationship so that our soul can have the experience of physicality and evolution.

Different traditions have different classifications and numbers of layers of the *koshas*. Most traditions have between four to seven distinctly different layers of the aura of our consciousness vehicle. They mostly describe them as the same but separate some layers into sublayers.

After looking at several philosophies, I have come to find great value in the Advaita Vedanta model of consciousness, as well as the contemporary models presented in Theosophy, the work of Meher Baba, and other lineages. The following theoretical model is a fusion combining the wisdom from my research.

Three-Body System

The human form can be separated into three different major bodies which can be separated into different planes of consciousness. The base for these layers is the Source Self which projects other layers to experience Creation. Note that I categorize these slightly differently than Vedanta. The three major layers are:

1. *Physical Body:* Physical, Material layer
2. *Subtle Body:* Etheric layer, conscious mind, subconscious
3. *Causal Body:* superconscious mind, buddhi, auric film

Some occult traditions break this into the categories of body, soul, and Spirit. The soul is the lightbody which is the combination of the subtle bodies and causal body from my model. This soul is what moves from life to life. The Spirit is the Atman/Self/Source, which is Absolute, omnipresent, omnipotent, and ever free. This is your True Nature.

The Causal Consciousness Body, the most subtle body is the first layer that manifests and is the seed layer from which the other layers emerge. It holds the karmic imprints and mental patterns from past lives which lie dormant until triggered by life experiences. The causal body gives birth to the subtle body, which create the template matrix for the physical body, which is the medium through which the soul experiences the Material Realm. In the model I use, the causal consciousness body includes the superconscious mind functions, the higher mind that is cultivated in spiritual awakening.

The Subtle Consciousness Body gives us the capacity to feel and sense our experience. This grouping of layers is made of the etheric structuring of the physical body as well as the functions of the conscious and subconscious mind. The subtle body gives us access to the subtle realms and bridges us with the higher consciousness planes. It is the layer in which universal *prana* enters our body and is converted for life processes. In some traditions, the life force layer (*pranamaya kosha*) is combined with the physical layer to create one "body of action." In other traditions, the pranic layer is considered part of the Subtle Body. I find understanding in both. For the sake of the ease of this transmission, I will link the vital layer with the Subtle Body.

According to Vedanta, the subtle body is said to have nineteen or seventeen main components, depending on the lineage of the teaching. In this system the higher and lower mind functions belong to the subtle body. The components include:

- five organs of knowledge (eyes, ears, nose, tongue, skin)
- five organs of action (mouth, hands, legs, genitals, anus),
- five pranas (*prana, apana, vyana, udana, samana*). I will also note the chakras and nadis here.
- four internal organs (mind/*manas*, memory/*chitta*, *intellect/*buddhi*, *ego/*ahamkara*).

The Physical Body exists in the physical plane. It is the densest layer and is made of all the physical organs, tissues, and their processes. It is the physical vehicle for soul, our subtle bodies, to experience physical life through. The transcendental Self, the Atman, pervades each layer, conducting the orchestration of all systems at once. Our True Nature, our True Self, is that One Light of Consciousness, the Awareness and Witness of all objects of experience including the bodymind and the world.

Within the three major bodies are the subplanes of each plane of existence with different functions that contribute to the whole. If there is curiosity, I recommend researching the lineages that I have sourced this wisdom from.

- **Physical Consciousness Body**
  - *Annamaya Kosha*: Physical Layer: Material Sheath
- **Subtle Consciousness Body**
  - *Pranamaya Kosha*: Vital Layer: Pranic Sheath
  - *Kamamaya Kosha*: Conscious Mind: Desire Sheath
  - *Manomaya Kosha*: Subconscious Mind: Mental Sheath
- **Causal Consciousness Body**
  - *Atimanasa Kosha*: Supramental Mind: Intuitive Sheath
  - *Vijnanamaya Kosha*: Subliminal Mind: Intellectual Sheath
  - *Anandamaya Kosha*: Subtle Causal Mind: Bliss Sheath
  - *Atman*: Pure Consciousness, Source within, Spirit

It is a common belief that we are a physical body that can have spiritual experiences, but the truth is we are a spiritual being that experiences ourselves in form. We originate beyond form and develop a causal body, subtle body, and physical body. In this way, we can think of these sheaths as layers of ignorance that distract us from perceiving the Atman/Source/Self, but they do not cover the Self because our True Nature is all-pervasive, vast, limitless, and unblockable. We just need to quiet the noise of the mind and senses to notice what is always there in the background of our awareness. We are Source right here, right now, and forever.

These coverings inhibit us from experiencing the knowledge of the Source Self. Our Source Self "sits" in the background witnessing the different bandwidths of density overlaying our Divine Nature. We are not the body that walks about this world of solid form. We are not the "breathing body" of vital energy and its vital processes. We are not the thinking consciousness, the egoic identity, or our memories and desires. We are not the intellectual processes of our higher mind. We are not even the blankness of the bliss consciousness. We are the Seer of all experiences. We are the pure Consciousness that observes them all. We are the Witness of these illusory phenomena, pure unbridled beingness. Through the process of Ascension, we are not rejecting the body or mind but elevating it to the highest capacity and functioning so that the full Light of our Being can shine through each kosha.

These sheaths are symbiotic, working together to create the vessel that you experience life through. These systems are always working toward harmony and vitality to create a resonant, unified field of pure light. This state of balance is called homeostasis, made through the harmonic organization and coherence of each sheath. As you come into deeper awareness of each layer and reconcile its distortions, the healing benefits spread to the other bodies so that the whole system benefits from improvements. This next section will take you through each of the koshas and provide thorough instructions on how to purify and strengthen each of these bodies in preparation for Ascension.

Moving from the Unreal to the Real

The koshas are the robes that Jesus spoke about when he taught of cleaning the robes to prepare for the next garment of Light. What we eat, what we give our life force to, and the thoughts we think affect our ability to tune into the brilliance of our Divine Nature.

Why do we not know our True Nature? We are confused and ignorant of our true beingness because of our misperceptions, misidentifications, and the roles connected to each of the koshas. Our awareness is focused on and distracted by our own *samsara*, our own suffering mind-body complex. We have become enamored and intoxicated by the dream spell of *maya.*

To understand our True Nature, to know what we ARE, we can negate or remove the layers of what we are NOT. As we peel back the layers of our *koshas* like we peel the layers of an onion, we arrive at the true knowledge of who we are as pure Consciousness.

In Advaita Vedanta there is an understanding that the True Nature is the Atman, the transcendental Self, which is Brahman (Source) having an experience in form as the individual self. The Atman is the Seer of Creation, so it can never be seen as an object or reduced to a form. It is the Atman, the Source within us, which gives us sentience, the awareness to witness the ever-shifting forms and names within one's experience. The pure Consciousness is stable, changeless, and ever-present. If your True Self is the subjective consciousness, sentient (aware), and changeless, we can test each of the *koshas* to see that they do not match these criteria. The physical body cannot be aware of the Source. The Etheric Body is constantly changing. The higher and lower mind faculties disappear in deep sleep and our experiences of bliss and unity come and go. Yet it is our self-luminous Self that shines the Light of awareness on all of these ever-shifting experiences.

The words we speak are like spells that can either move us into higher states of expansion or they can anchor us into the illusion even more. Every time we say the words "I am..." the words that follow have an immediate effect and can show us which layer of our personality we are identifying with. When we say, "I am ugly," we are identifying with the physical body. When we say, "I am exhausted," we are identifying with our vital energy system. When we say, "I am mad," we are identifying with the emotional body. "I am confused," we are identifying with the mental body. Yet, all the while, the soul still shines as Pure Consciousness. A more accurate statement would be "I am pure consciousness experiencing this body, vitality, and the manifestations of thought and insight." You are ever the witness and never the witnessed. You are pure consciousness itself!

When we get our awareness overly involved in the different layers of our personality, their roles, and the manifestations in those layers, we overlook our Divine Self. It is a paradox in that the spiritual journey is one of seeking and looking for the "Truth of Who I Am," yet Source is always there. Our True Self is always present, yet most of humanity consciously or unconsciously decides to "look the other way" and gets caught up in associating with the distractions of the different layers of density that make up the koshas. Yet, at some point we "hear the call" of our divine nature saying "Come, find me." and the spiritual journey begins. We begin to remember the mission of ascension that we planned for ourselves before we entered this physical world. We begin to turn away from the "ways of the world" and begin to seek fulfillment from living a spiritualized life focused on awakening to the True Nature of reality.

How do we free ourselves from our limited egoic identity, spiritual ignorance, and karmic prison? There are infinite ways! Every spiritual wisdom tradition has ways of focusing one's life towards the Higher Consciousness. The yogic sciences encourage us to fine-tune our awareness and action towards altruistic actions that serve the good of all (*karma yoga*). We can balance the polarities of our bodymind complex (*hatha yoga*). We can grow in devotion to and our love of God (*bhakti yoga*). We can meditate on our Divine Nature and the Divine Reality (*raja yoga*). We can infuse our minds with Divine Knowledge (*jnana yoga*). While these names are Sanskrit terms, similar concepts can be found in all wisdom and faith traditions.

From the perspective of linear time, our many incarnations evolved our individual consciousness by progressing from the simplest to most complex consciousness forms to the point of taking human form. In human form, we can begin the process of liberating our consciousness in what is called God-realization, Self-realization, or Ascension. Even though the divine presence of our True Being is always there, yet it requires seeking, searching, and spiritual practice to fully establish ourselves in that pure Consciousness state. For most, it takes many lifetimes to fully realize what we have always been.

It is said at the highest state of realization, we live in the knowing that we were never caught in karma, we were never born and never died. All was just an appearance, a game of Light and shadow we played with our Oneself. We have always been free, we are free, and we will always be free we just have not yet noticed it through direct experience and embodied knowledge.

The next portion of the book takes you deeper into each layer so that you can uncover the treasure that lies within the core of your being and permeates every atom of your physical form. As we journey through these layers of our personality, we find that the Kingdom of Heaven lives within our very being! Take a moment to still the body and quiet the mind and listen to your inner dimension and see what is already there. What you seek is closer than you think.

SEVEN

Annamaya Kosha: Physical Body

When most people think of who they are, they think of the physical body. This is the matter, muscles, skin, bones, connective tissues, organs, blood, cells, DNA, etc. The physical vessel is transient and passes through the stages of birth, growth, degeneration, and physical death. The *annamaya kosha* is related to the Root Chakra, your physical DNA, and your maternal and paternal ancestral lines. This dense energy envelope is made of the food you eat and is the vehicle for our Source Self to experience physicality. At the base level of the physical body, you find the five elemental energies of earth, water, fire, air, and space/ether which organize in countless ways to create things like bone structure, bodily fluids, digestive power, movement of breath, and the space that surrounds and separates the many parts and systems of the body. This body is not who we truly are. From ashes to ashes, dust to dust, five elements to five elements it will go. Yet, we are eternal.

Experiencing the Matrix of Existence

Our movement through the activities of our life is powered through a multidimensional exchange of energy information. Energy information passes through the physical sense organs of our eyes, skin, ears, tongue, nose and brain which give us the perceptual power to experience the subtle elements of form, touch, sound, taste, and smell. As this energy information is processed from the physical body into the subtle body via the etheric structuring of the *pranamaya kosha*. It is then directed into the mind where it is experienced, processed, and stored. Almost immediately impulses of desire and willpower ripple out through the mind into the vital energy structures and our physical brain and body to direct physical processes and the organs of action which include the mouth, hands, feet, excretory organs, and reproductive organs.

The physical vessel is constantly receiving energy information and transforming it into useful data for the body systems. The systems of the physical body include the skeletal, muscular, nervous, endocrine, respiratory, reproductive, immune, urinary, digestive, circulatory, cardiovascular, lymphatic, and integumentary systems. This complex network of systems is always working towards harmony and balance called homeostasis.

Illness and Disease

Physical illness is a manifestation of dense, toxic energy eliminated through the symptoms of the illness. The root of all illness, disorder, and disease can be found in the subtle bodies as manifestation is always energetic before it becomes physical. We think a certain way, which energizes our body into speech and action which move us into situations of balance or imbalance, health or disease. Even hereditary illness is an echo of thoughts and karmic actions passed down through our genetic lineages and humanity's collective unconscious. Latent mental patterning stored in the Causal Body can also be reactivated by our environment causing us to recreate injuries and illness from past lives.

Our health is affected by the things we see, the quality of the air we breathe, the things we eat, the sounds we hear, and the things we put on our skin. We are inundated with toxins from our environment and distorted programming from the mainstream industries. Many people live in areas of pollution and eat poisonous food. Finding natural solutions and detoxifying our bodies is essential for Ascension to ensure a clean and clear Ascension vessel, the physical body.

Understanding Stress

One of the major causes of physical body imbalance is stress. Stress is a feeling of mental, emotional, or physical tension that occurs as we face the challenges of living. In some cases, stress can be healthy and drive us to accomplish our goals. Stress can also be detrimental to our health, such as enduring traumatic conditions or unhealthy mental pressure from the conditioning of the mind.

Stress and anxiety wreak havoc on the systems of our body and consciousness. Erratic emotions, body tension, fearful thinking, and unhealthy behavioral patterns are symptoms of us being out of balance.

Mindfulness and wellness practices move our bodymind systems out of stagnation and decay into regenerative states of cohesion, balance, and flow.

Stress, real or imagined, has an immediate effect on all body systems, including the nervous system, digestive system, reproductive system, respiratory system, mental cognition, and so on. One of the keys to understanding stress and stress management is through the autonomic nervous system. Following is a summary of the components and functions of our autonomic nervous system and how we create stress or harmony through our physiology.

Autonomic Nervous System

The autonomic nervous system (ANS) regulates bodily functions such as breathing rate, heart rate, digestion, urination, and pupillary response. This system helps us adjust to daily living demands from a place of stress and anxiety or a place of flow and balance. The ANS acts mostly unconsciously and has two subsystems that create the "fight, flight, or freeze" responses of the body (sympathetic nervous system) or the "rest and digest" response (parasympathetic nervous system).

Sympathetic Nervous System

The sympathetic nervous system (SNS) is activated when the body and mind are under stress. This could be from actual stressors in our environment like toxins, loud noises, or stressful situations. This can also happen when the mind drifts into memories of past stress or projects stressful outcomes in the future.

When our sympathetic nervous system is activated, our digestive system stops working, and the blood is redirected to the arms and legs so that we can fight our stress or run from it. In this stage of ANS response, our heart rate elevates and becomes erratic. When our body and mind are in various stress states, we switch from deeper diaphragmatic breathing to shallow upper chest breathing as the sympathetic nervous system activates.

With the diaphragm frozen in movement, the upper chest and neck muscles pull on the rib cage to make space for the lungs to expand. This results in shorter, shallow breathing that leaves our neck and chest muscles tight and agitated. Our autonomic nervous system often stays in fight or flight response way after the initial stressful experience partly because the respiratory system stays locked in defense mode while our subconscious stores the unprocessed energy information. This creates trapped emotions that continue to oscillate in one's mental field creating tremors of reactivation within the bodymind complex.

Modern Western society is a product of the SNS where everyone is fighting to survive or climb an invisible social ladder. We are inundated with blatant and subliminal messages that we are not enough, and our future is bleak. This constant stress manifests as chronic illness, emotional disorders, and beyond. One of the most radical things you can do to unplug from this machine's momentum is to develop mindful breathing and presence.

Parasympathetic Nervous System

When our parasympathetic nervous system (PNS) is activated, our heart rate slows down, our breathing deepens, our digestive system runs smoothly, and our overall mood and mind are balanced. When our body and mind are calm and relaxed, we naturally use our diaphragm for breathing, allowing our lower abdomen to expand and contract. This movement and type of breathing are easily seen by observing an infant or sleeping dog.

Diaphragmatic breathing is natural and effortless for the body. The diaphragm, like the heart, can continue contracting and releasing without tiring or needing rest. When we practice diaphragmatic breathing, our respiratory organs and digestive organs are massaged, cleansed, and toned by the rhythmic movement caused by the expansion of the diaphragm and lungs.

Vagus Nerve

The vagus nerve system of neural pathways originates in the brain stem and weaves a serpentine pathway through the body, touching upon various vital organs and neural networks before it fractals out into the intestines. This family of neural pathways interacts with the *hara line/sushumna and* chakras to send information to the brain to modulate emotions, translate intuitive "gut" instincts, create bodily sensations, inform relationship responses, and activate processes for environmental adaptation.

The Dance of the Autonomic Nervous System

The vagus nerve plays a significant part in transferring from the SNS (sympathetic nervous system) to the PNS (parasympathetic nervous system). "Vagal tone" is our ability to respond to stressors in our life. When the vagal tone is low and unhealthy, we are quickly agitated and stressed out by life. When the vagal tone is high and healthy, we can quickly and easily manage life stressors and return to the states of homeostasis and flow.

Activities for increasing vagal tone: dancing, yoga, meditation, massage, singing, chanting, prayer, cold exposure (cold shower), positive social connections, and other relaxing and inspiring activities.

We are constantly shifting in and out of PNS and SNS responses. Both the SNS and PNS are activated within a single breath cycle. As we inhale, the SNS activates, causing our heart rate to increase. We feel alert, active, and inspired during the inhalation phase. As we exhale, the PNS activates, causing our heart rate to lower and the vagal response to increase. As we exhale, we soften, relax, and settle into ourselves. There is nothing wrong or bad about the SNS, we just should not live there out of habit, or we will likely fry our systems.

Conscious breathing directs our mental awareness to our experience of breathing, where we can become conscious influencers of our autonomic nervous system. When we link our awareness with our breath, we almost automatically switch to calmer, deeper breathing, and a more balanced state of being. As our parasympathetic nervous system activates through conscious, diaphragmatic breathing, all our body systems begin to balance and restore.

When someone takes a "sigh of relief," this is the bodymind complex releasing the physical, vital, and mental responses to the stressful experience. Deep sighs of relief are signs that the ANS is switching from SNS to a PNS response. Walking in nature, meditation, physical exercise, and spending quiet time alone all help the PNS activate and restore our body systems to homeostasis, coherence, and flow.

One of the best ways to increase vagal tone and increase our vital energy is through conscious embodiment practices like meditation and yoga. Conscious breathing practices are simple tools we can use to regulate subtle energy in our body systems and establish states of rejuvenation and calm presence. These are spoken of more in the *pranamaya kosha* section, and the mental component of stress is discussed more deeply in the section on the *manomaya kosha*.

Physical Body Focuses for Ascension

The physical layer of our personality will be transforming with us as we transmigrate from this dimensional reality to the next. The biological and subtle energy processes of ascension need nourishment to ensure an easy transition. Below are a few keys regarding the physical layer maintenance through the ascension process.

Physical Body Training

Physical training and self-care should incorporate a balance of active and passive activities to regulate the autonomic nervous system, develop overall strength and flexibility, and reduce stress and neuromuscular tension.

For those who tend to have higher levels of stress and body tension, passive practices such as restorative yoga, self-massage, sound healing, journaling, and long baths can be added to activate the parasympathetic nervous response to calm the bodymind. Long, gentle stretching helps to loosen the connective tissues of the body to create harmonic flow in the physical and subtle body systems.

For those who need to develop strength and willpower, active practices such as working out at the gym, martial arts, hatha yoga, and brisk walking help to energize and strengthen the body. Active practices help to develop muscle tone, increase coordination and create movement in the organs and tissues of the body for healthy elimination and detoxification.

Overall, each individual's practices and life activities should be a balance between movement and stillness, active and passive, fast and slow to bring the bodymind systems into harmony and cohesion.

Self-Massage Practice

There are a variety of ways to do self-massage. Here is a short description of a self-massage practice to improve circulation, balance overall skin health, reduce stress, and so much more. Go slow. Enjoy the sensuality and use it as a practice of devotion towards yourself, your body, and beyond.

1. Use warmed organic oils like coconut oil, sesame, or something similar. You may wish to use organic essential oils as well.
2. Start at the scalp and work your way down to the collarbone. Use the fingertips to make tiny circles. Pay special attention to Crown, Brow, Zeal, and Throat Chakras.
3. Progress from fingertips to shoulder with long strokes on the limbs and short, circular strokes at the joints. Repeat on the other arm.
4. Employ the same concept from feet to hips.
5. Massage the abdomen with clockwise strokes.
6. Massage across the low back/sacral.
7. Rub center of the chest outward.
8. Pause for 5-10 minutes. Bonus if you use Reiki on yourself or meditate during that time.
9. Rinse with a cold/cool shower.

Diet and Water Intake

Every human body is different in what it needs to sustain itself through this process. Whatever you ingest, try your best to have organic foods that are grown locally and ethically. It has been suggested that we eliminate dairy because it creates a distortion in the energy layers that makes energy upgrades difficult. Plant-based diets are most recommended but if you must eat meat, make sure the animal was raised humanely and organically. Be sure to give thanks to the life expression of that being for its sacrifice.

Foods should be living and fresh, not processed or from cans. Supplements are recommended to ensure that you are getting all the nutrients that you need. Superfoods that have high nutritional value help keep everything vibrant and healthy.

Water is super important for the alchemical transformation of Ascension. Spring water or from other pure natural water sources is the best, and it is recommended to add hydration salts and trace minerals if using purified water. Municipal water sources should be avoided as the water is most likely highly contaminated with chemicals that negatively affect the body and mind.

It is recommended to perform intermittent fasting and periodic detoxification protocols to rid the body of toxic waste. These are excellent to start around the full moon as the waning movement helps with the release of physical, energetic, and mental patterns that are not of the highest benefit to your well-being.

Take time to pray over your food. Hold your hands above the food and envision Light shining from your hands and/or your brow chakra to enhance and purify the food. Send gratitude to all the forces and beings that played a part in bringing you your meal. Eat mindfully, slowly, and allow yourself to have a multidimensional experience as you eat.

Proper Rest and Sleep

Proper rest is important for optimal physical, vital, and mental well-being. Everyone is different with how many hours are needed for rest. Find ways to increase the length of time in the blankness of deep sleep. This includes limiting screen time before bed and reducing the amount of stimulants and caffeine taken into the body. Have a self-reflection and winding down practice to get the body ready for rest. This will help to clear the mind so that you are not too active in dream states and can spend more time in the state of dreamless sleep.

Progressive Relaxation Body Scan

Progressive relaxation practices help develop body consciousness and an overall feeling of deep relaxation. The fascial grid is a network of connective tissue that surrounds all the muscles, organs, tendons, and even the bones. Our bodies have many habitual holding patterns which limit the free flow of subtle energy throughout our system. The fascial grid acts as a passageway for vital energy. Holding patterns in any area of the grid limit the free flow of vital energy and cause disruption and imbalance. As you practice this body scan, imagine the whole fascial network softening to allow the free flow of subtle energy.

Progressive Relaxation Body Scan Procedure

- Lay down or recline in a comfortable position.
- Breathe into the naval center, diaphragmatic breathing, for a few rounds to settle into your body.

- Feel the breath in the throat for a few rounds and set intention to relax the bodymind.
- Breath into the nostrils and allow yourself to settle into even deeper subtle consciousness. Take this profound feeling of relaxation and focus throughout the body scan. Take your time and enjoy the process.
- Relax the scalp and crown of your head.
- Relax the muscles of your face.
- Relax the forehead, eyebrows, and eyes.
- Relax your cheeks, tongue, mouth, jaw, chin, throat, and neck.
- Relax your shoulders, upper arms, elbows, lower arms, wrists, hands, and fingers (rest for five breaths).
- Relax your heart center and sides of chest
- Relax your solar plexus and stomach.
- Relax your lower abdomen, pelvis, pubic bone, pelvic floor, and lower back.
- Relax your upper legs, lower legs, ankles, feet, and toes (waiting here for five breaths).
- Reverse the process back up to the crown without pausing. Relax for several breaths and slowly return to waking consciousness by deepening the breath and moving the fingertips and toes tips.

Bless Your Body

Before incarnation, you chose the perfect genetics to experience this life through. Love this physical body and treat it well as it is the temple of your Divine Light. Celebrate the body and dedicate it towards your higher purpose, using it as an instrument for your liberation. Enjoy your senses; enjoy your path; and dedicate your physical vessel's life expressions towards the liberation of all beings from cycles of suffering!

EIGHT

Pranamaya Kosha: Pranic Body

In the beginning stages of spiritual awakening, we begin to realize that there is something more to physical life than what can be experienced with the physical senses and mainstream reality structure. We begin to sense something mystical to life and begin to turn inward to listen to our inner realm and tune into the interconnectedness of life.

As we awaken, we begin to discover that we exist within a unified field of light and vibration, a continuum of energy that is constantly shifting and changing through an infinite latticework of geometric grid patterns which mesh together to create the holographic matrix of the universe. When I use the word 'energy' throughout this book, subtle energy is what I speak of. Subtle energies are the substratum of all manifestations in Creation and act as the organizing principle, providing the pathways and movements of Consciousness as it evolves within the Unified Field of Creation. Subtle energy is interactive with our own consciousness. As we focus on it, it begins to transform immediately as it links with our consciousness giving us the ability to transfer will and intent across time and space such as in prayer and psychic phenomena.

It should be mentioned that not all energy is "good energy." There are seemingly negative, entropic energies that take away life force, and there are positive, centropic energies that sustain and revitalize life. These energies aren't "good" or "bad" as each frequency serves a purpose or function. The "problem" with energy comes when things are out of sync with Natural Order and are not able to balance and integrate back into wholeness.

In Samkhya, dualistic Vedic philosophy, there is the pure Self, *purusha*, and matter and form, *prakriti. Prakriti, maya* consists of three fundamental forces: *sattva, rajas,* and *tamas.* These forces called *gunas,* translated as "strand" or "fiber," are the threads that weave the web of the manifestation of the cosmos. All phenomena that can be experienced, seen and unseen, is a manifestation of the weaving of the matrix with the force of the *gunas in conjunction with the subtle and gross elements of earth, air, fire, water, and ether (space).*

These forces can be described as follows:

- *sattva*: harmony, purity, light, beauty, balance, consciousness revelation, balance, inspiration
- *rajas*: change, activity, active energy, unsteadiness, movement, agitation, transitions us to sattvic or tamasic
- *tamas*: darkness, conceals consciousness, ignorance, depression, dullness, stagnation, inertia, stability, mindless, intoxicating, inaction

All of these forces can be positive when in balance with the other forces. Ultimately, we should be guiding our experience into sattvic states of balance and inspiration versus the downward spirals that leads to ignorance, decay, and stagnation.

Most ancient cultures have various ways of accessing, manipulating, and understanding the many subtle energy categories and their qualities. There are many names in many cultures for subtle energy. *Ki* (Japanese), *prana* (Sanskrit), *chi* (Chinese), *ruach* (Hebrew), and *life force energy* (English) are just a few.

Prana is the animating life force of the physical body and the active power behind all vital phenomena in the universe. We receive this "breath of life" from the food and water we ingest, our environment, our inhalations of breath, and from our soul and higher consciousness connection. While *prana* is necessary for biological life to exist, too much of it causes nervousness and psychosis and in the most extreme case death. Having too little of it causes exhaustion, and our physical life is over when there is no longer *prana* in the physical body.

Alchemical practices like tantra, yoga, qi gong, and the laying of hands work with subtle energy to restore balance and harmony to a person's physical, vital, and mental bodies to create homeostasis and alignment with one's True Nature. Group prayer and ceremonies create a powerful energy field that amplifies prayers and intentions, and many people experience spontaneous healing and emotional healing through the group prayer field.

Many people who have not had a subtle energy experience of their own find it hard to believe that subtle energy exists, believing in only what they see with their physical eyes. Many reject the idea of a subtle energy reality. Scientific communities are beginning to develop instruments that can measure subtle energy. Many hospitals and clinics in the West are now beginning to allow practitioners of acupuncture and hands-on healing methods like Reiki into the hospital system to support patients' recovery.

Simple Energy Exercise

One of the best tools to sense and interact with subtle energy is with the hands. The awareness is amplified when you apply conscious breathing to the task.

Bring your palms together and begin to rub them vigorously while you consciously breathe in and out of your belly. Close your eyes and feel the sensations. Intend to generate powerful energy and heat. Use your breath and intention to amplify the vibrations, intending for the energy field to grow stronger and brighter. After a few moments, begin to open your hands slowly. Tune into the sensations between your hands. What do you feel? What do you sense? Trust your feelings. Can you feel both the electric and magnetic qualities? Warm or cold sensations? Tingling? This is a form of subtle energy. You can take your hands and lightly move them across your face and body and sense the energy there. When finished, keep the awareness, and open the eyes.

The Human Energy System

Inserted in the physical body and extending slightly beyond is the vital body, also called the etheric body or pranic body. The human body is a multidimensional bio-transducer, meaning it constantly receives, transforms, and emits various levels of subtle energy. The vital energy system translates energy information into the physical systems to create physical body functions like heart rate, hormone release, breathing rate, and beyond. This sheath bridges our physical body with our mental body by translating subtle energy information for physical and mental processes.

In Theosophy, this layer is called the Etheric Body Double because it is similar in shape and size to the physical body. Every cell of the body, every particle of bodily fluids, bodily gas, and organic material is surrounded by an etheric energy envelope that weaves a matrix of pathways to unify all systems. As information streams in through the physical sense experiences, information is passed from the cells into the etheric double of the cells and is translated through subtle information pathways to the etheric brain and mental body. Higher consciousness information and mental patterning experienced in the mental body are transmitted through the etheric pathways and etheric brain into the physical brain and nervous system to direct the body's actions and functions.

Aura: Your Personal Space

All living organisms have an auric field which is called a biofield in science. The human biofield is a toroidal field of electromagnetic light that emanates from the core of your being and creates the matrix framework for your physical body. The aura includes the etheric structuring of the *pranamaya kosha* as well as the oscillation and activities of the mental and causal bodies. Our aura is multilayered and is in constant evolution and transformation based on our mood, thoughts, the food we eat, location, etc. Our auric field is the instrument we use to interact with the subtle energy world around us. It receives energy information from outside of our physical body and radiates energy information into the Unified Field of Creation. Our overall light quotient in our auric field is dependent on the health of all our koshas. Our auric field becomes unstable and distorted when we are in states of aggression, sadness, or other lower emotions. Our auric field is harmoniously organized and coherent when we are in higher vibrational states like joy, creativity, and devotion.

Aura Experience

Close your eyes and begin to focus on your breath and the subtle sensations of your experience. Call the Light to be with you and feel your vibration begin to rise. Imagine that within your heart center, in the core of your being, is a sacred fire, a beautiful bright Light of Source Energy. Use your intention, focus, and breathing to expand this source of energy until it surrounds you. Make your space feel beautiful and loving and filled with light. Deep, full breathing amplifies the radiance and love from this Light. Allow your thoughts to be purified and your mind relaxed by this Light. Feel your intention to merge with the Light and evoke feelings of peace and tranquility. Amplify these positive sensations with your breathing. Notice how far your personal energy field goes. Is it a bubble or does it fade out into the space around you? Feel the energy within you. Notice any stagnant areas, and breathe light and awareness into them, inviting movement and flow.

As you inhale, pull your field back into the core of your being. As you exhale, pulse your light back out. Keep repeating this pattern as if you are flexing your etheric muscles. With each exhale, your aura is brighter, cleaner, and more pronounced. Enjoy this for as long as you desire. When you are complete, feel your aura strong and illuminated. Feel blessed by the experience and open your eyes.

Boundaries

It is important to do frequent aura clearing and restructuring throughout the day, especially if you live a hectic life. Having healthy, energetic boundaries ensures that we do not take on the energy of other people and places. Having a clear aura helps you to have clear thoughts and a joyful mood. Practices like smudging or spraying "aura mists" over the body help to clear and recharge the energy field. It is especially important to intentionally restructure and strengthen your energy field when you go into public so that you remain sovereign and clear of others' energy.

Five Movements of the Breath of Life

We access and regulate the *pranamaya kosha* through the act of breathing, our main source of *prana,* and intentionally through the power of our mind. As this universal life force enters our body it is separated into five "winds" with different movement patterns and functions. These five pranic winds stimulate all bodily processes and govern our health and vitality. Any disruptions or imbalances in the flow of these life force patterns manifest on both the physical and mental planes of our personality. The five major movements of *prana* in the body are as follows:

One: Incoming Energy

Prana vayu, located in the region of the head and chest, moves inward and upward and deals with inspiration, intake, receptivity, and forward momentum and is associated with the heart chakra and brow chakra and the air element. Prana enters through the organs of perception from the food we eat, the air we breathe, the sights we see, the sounds we hear, and through the skin. Imbalances may present as dysfunction in the lungs, heart, brain, and circulatory system.

Two: Outgoing Energy

Apana vayu, located in the pelvic region and lower abdomen, expels downward and outward, deals with elimination movements like perspiration, defecation, and urination. It directs the reproductive processes of ejaculation, menstruation, and childbirth and is associated with the organs below the naval. It is associated with the *muladhara chakra*, the Root Center, and the earth element. Imbalances manifest as dysfunction in organs of elimination and reproduction.

Three: Digestive Energy

Samana vayu, located between the navel and heart, is the balancing energy of the body which deals with multidimensional digestion and assimilation processes and is associated with the *manipura chakra*, the solar plexus, and the element of fire. *Samana vayu* draws energy into the solar plexus center for processing our food, subtle energy, thoughts, and energy from the physical holographic reality. Imbalances can manifest as over or underactive digestive patterns, abdominal discomfort, and gas.

Four: Upward Energy

Udana vayu, located in the throat, has an upward movement and deals with speech, expression, growth, and the upward ascension of prana and kundalini. Associated with the *vishuddha chakra*, *udana vayu* emanates from the throat center in a circular motion around the neck and head, thus assisting with mental clarity and focus. It directs the self-transformation process and the recalibration of willpower to a higher purpose and vision. Imbalances manifest as dysfunction in the throat, neck, and head.

Five: Circulation Energy

Vyana vayu, located in and around the whole body, has an outward from center movement pattern and deals with circulation, expansiveness, and pervasiveness as it directs subtle energy throughout the 72,000 pathways of subtle energy called *nadis* which physicalize as communication networks like the nerves and fascial grid. This movement provides a connection between the senses, nerves, tissues, cells, and the mind creating a feeling of wholeness and containment. This circulatory movement is associated with the *svadhisthana chakra*, the sacral center, and the element of water. Imbalances manifest as feeling unstable, containerless, and clumsy. Overall, the imbalance manifests as systemic dysfunctions of the body

There is an ancient saying that says something like, "If you can extend the length of your breath, you can extend the length of your life." Our quality of breathing, from day to day, determines our quality of living. As we train the breath, we become more radiant and vital. Many spiritual and mystical traditions revere the transformative power of the breath. Life can be thought of as one long breath cycle starting from the first inhalation as a newborn to the last breath of life. Breathing transforms our experience of time. Fast, shallow breathing is parallel to the experience of rush or not enough time. Slow and steady breathing brings us to the present moment where time endlessly unfolds in the eternal NOW.

Hara Line: Bridging Heaven and Earth

You are connected to universal life force and the regenerative consciousness field of Gaia by a pillar of Light that passes through the center of the body, which I call the hara line or pranic tube, or the sushumna nadi when speaking about the physical body. This pranic tube is the axis of the toroidal field of your auric field.

This subtle energy tube tethers us to the subtle planes and the electromagnetic fields of planet Earth. This is our lifeline and our connection to our battery. When we are in the states of love and trust, this pathway is open and clear. When we are in the states of fear and separation consciousness, we are severed from our battery, and we lose life force.

Our hara line, our pranic tube, is the main intake and outtake pathway of our subtle energy body and supplies our chakras with energy from Source and Gaia. When we have a healthy hara line, we feel centered in our being, connected to Source and Gaia, and alive and aligned with our Divine Purpose and the Divine Will of the Universe. We feel energized, alert, and connected to Higher Love.

When our hara line is distorted and blocked, we can feel a myriad of physical, mental, emotional, and spiritual issues. In my opinion, most, if not all, issues stem from hara line distortions and misalignment since the chakras also lay on this major pathway.

Pranic Tube Meditation

Sit or stand so that your spine is erect, and you feel comfortable. Begin to breathe into your hara line and heart until you feel calm and present. Imagine that there is a shining, golden-white star far above your head. This will symbolize your Source, God/Goddess/All That Is.

Invite and imagine that a flowing stream of energy flows down from Source and passes through your crown, all the way through the body, and down into the Earth. Breath this Source Light into your Hara, into your womb, filling it with pure, clear, golden-white energy. Exhale and send the energy down into the Earth. Repeat this breathing pattern a few times and allow this pure Source Energy to sweep away any stagnant or dense energy and release it down into the Earth to be composted. This will not harm the planet. She lovingly takes all our sorrows and struggles and transforms them for us.

Bring your hands onto your heart and feel your own heart's energy. Breathe into it and help it shine. Intend to sense Gaia's heart. Intend to connect to her pulsating rhythm of love. Begin to breathe her love and evolutionary coding up through your hara line into your own heart. Fill your heart with this love and as you exhale, send this love back to Source. Continue a few more times, breathing all this love up into the body and feel Gaia's heart, your heart, and the heart of Creation flowing together and synchronizing.

Bring your hands down to your lap and breathe normally. Sense what has shifted and enjoy your moment. When you are finished, feel blessed to have this connection and open your eyes.

Pranic Tube Tune-Up and Boundaries

Throughout the day, you can clear out your hara line and realign with your Divine Purpose. Simply use conscious breathing, intention, and imagination. As you inhale, bring the energy down from Source into your hara channeling down the Divine Presence, then exhale, grounding the energy into Gaia. Inhale drawing earth energy up from the core of Gaia into your heart. Exhale, send the energy back to Source fully establishing the bridge. Inhale from Gaia and Source, then exhale, radiating light outward, re-establishing your field's boundaries. Make your entire "breathing space" illuminated with compassionate presence. Repeat the pattern until you reach the desired state of stability, peace, and wholeness. In just three breath cycles, you can completely refresh and revitalize your entire energy system and your consciousness and avoid unnecessary suffering.

Nadis

Nadis, Sanskrit for "river channel," are pathways for our subtle energy to move throughout our bioelectric system. The physical manifestation of the nadis include the nerves and fascial grid. Some ancient texts say that there are over 72,000 nadis that weave a matrix of light around and within your body that lead to every cell of your physicality. The three major nadis as called *ida, pingala,* and *sushumna.*

Ida and Pingala

Ida and *pingala nadis,* related to the vagus nerves, represent the feminine and masculine polarities of our personality. These two serpent energies weave through our chakra system to create conduits of consciousness that meet in the Brow Center. These two energy pathways play such an important role in health and wellness that the symbol of the *caduceus* has been used by the medical/healing world for a long time. This symbol is depicted as the wand that Hermes or Mercury carries in Greek and Roman mythology.

Ida nadi, the feminine pathway, starts in the root chakra on the left and weaves its way up through the chakras finishing at our left nostril at the brow center. Often associated with the moon, this feminine energy is considered reflective, intuitive, cooling, and nurturing and is described as the mental force, *manas shakti.* This current is active when the left nostril is flowing, and the right hemisphere of the brain is active.

Pingala nadi, the masculine pathway, begins at the root chakra on the right and weaves its way up through the chakras finishing at the right nostril at the brow center. Often associated with solar qualities, this masculine power directs life force energy, *prana shakti,* to energize all essential life processes and is related to heat, logic, assertiveness, and action. This current is active when the right nostril is flowing, and the left-brain hemisphere is activated.

As we breathe in and out through our nose, air carries subtle energy through these two pathways to clear and revitalize the chakra system. As we switch between our consciousness's masculine and feminine qualities, one or the other pathways become dominant. Although without balance and awareness, we can either overstress our energy systems or become lethargic.

The most direct and transformative way I know to balance the masculine and feminine qualities of our consciousness is through the alternate nostril breathing technique, *nadi shodhanam,* and the system of hatha yoga. That being said, all effective healing and personal transformational processes inherently involve the balancing of these polarities.

Sushumna Nadi and Kundalini Shakti

The *sushumna* is the part of our hara line related to our physical body and the seven-chakra system. This tube of light charges and energizes the chakra system. It runs from the base of the spine at the perineum up to the crown of the head. At the base of the *sushumna*, wrapped around the base of the spine, lies the *kundalini shakti*, the ecstatic expression and spiritual potential of your spiritual being.

The *kundalini* energy is said to sit coiled at the base of the spine in *muladhara chakra,* the Root Center. As a soul progresses through incarnations, certain interactions begin to activate this dormant energy and it begins to rise up through *sushumna* balancing the polarities of each chakra as it makes its upward ascension. These two polarities eventually join at the Brow Center to create an experience that some call *Hieros Gamos,* which refers to this alchemical unification of the twin flame polarities within which is the goal of *hatha yoga* practices. Once this has occurred, *kundalini* can make its full ascension to the Crown Center to create the experience called *moksha, nirvana,* salvation, or any of the other names which describe fully realized Godself Consciousness.

Kundalini awakening can be felt like a surge of electrical current from the root of the spine into the higher energy centers of the brow and crown chakras. This can be experienced with body tremors, waves of wisdom and insight, waves of ecstasy, spontaneous mudras and positionings of the body, big emotional shifts, visionary experiences, sensory overload, and more.

Kundalini shakti, the ecstatic, spiritual potential within one's consciousness, begins to rise up the spine and activate each chakra and balance the consciousness at each center on its ascension towards the crown. For most people, *kundalini* rises and then goes back to rest in the Root Center while the practitioner reconciles their consciousness. Progress in one life carries over to the next life. Many "spiritual people" or those on the awakening path have had *kundalini* activation in previous lives and will continue this lifetime working in the chakra that they left off with in the "previous" incarnation. It is said that most of those on the "spiritual path" have at least activated the first three chakras and are beginning to work towards the heart chakra.

As humanity ascends, the awakening of the serpent energies can be quite powerful and intoxicating. As we heal and integrate our consciousness's masculine and feminine qualities, we awaken and stir our creative, sexual-spiritual energies. It is important to learn practices of grounding to work with these energies effectively and safely.

Ascension alchemy practices like Ancient Egyptian sex magic, true tantra, and kundalini and hatha yoga are designed to awaken these energy systems, purify them, and unify our consciousness with the Absolute. While it can be intoxicating and exhilarating to stay in states of kundalini activation, it is also important to ingest foods and participate in activities that nourish and soothe our nervous systems so that we do not "burn out" or overstress them. I recommend seeking out a teacher or a guide who can safely guide you through kundalini awakening if you are feeling unstable through your awakening process.

Chakras: Lenses to See the World

Emerging from *sushumna* channel, we have the blooming of seven main energy vortexes commonly known as the "*chakras.*" The chakra system goes by different names in different traditions. These seals/wheels/lamps/vortices tether our physical body with our subtle body processes. They are toroidal in shape and always in states of movement and evolution. They contain life force energy as well as mental energy. Like individual minds, each contains our programmed beliefs about the seven major areas of our life, such as community and physical life, self-identity and relationships, willpower, compassion, communication, vision, and universality. Besides the seven main chakras, there are many sub-chakras and micro-chakras throughout the body with some existing outside of the body. However, these seven are the most important when cultivating consciousness liberation and holistic wellness.

Each of the seven main chakras relates to certain glands in the endocrine system, nerve plexi, and particular organs and bodily systems. As energy information passes through the aura, it is processed through the chakra system and creates emotional/mental/physical experiences based on our beliefs and previous experiences with similar dynamics. This energy ripples out across the subtle energy pathways (nadis/meridians) into the nervous system and endocrine system to create sensations, bodily functions, and events.

Chakra Locations

Here are the locations of the seven main chakras, the two minor chakras, and the three newly emerging ascension chakras:

- **Soul Star Center:** Felt 6-12 inches above the head
- **Crown Center:** Crown of the head
- **Brow Center:** Between the forehead and occiput
- **Zeal Center:** Emanating from the medulla oblongata, attachment point of the spine to the skull
- **Throat Center:** Center of the throat
- **Heart Center:** Felt between and behind the manubrium and xiphoid process of the sternum
- **Solar Plexus Center:** Just below the diaphragm
- **Sacral Center:** Low abdomen behind the naval
- **Root Center:** Base of the spine at the pelvic floor
- **Earth Star Center:** Below the feet when standing, below the pelvis when seated
- **Palm Chakras:** Center of the palms
- **Foot Chakras:** Soles of the feet

Chakra Filaments: How We Feel Our Environment

Chakras radiate filaments of light, just like the rays and filaments of the sun. The number of filaments on a chakra relates to the frequency of the chakra. The higher the frequency, the higher the number of petals opening from the electromagnetic flower.

These filaments reach out to interact with a specific layer of our auric field. Picture a plasma ball from science class with the violet plasma whipping across the inside of the glass globe. Each filament reaches through its environment to absorb the energy information in the world around us while simultaneously broadcasting our essence into the field. The chakras respond to our attention. As we focus our energy on an object, they begin to drink in the energy of the object of our attention.

Attachments and Cords

When we develop an attachment to an object, our energy forms a habit of focusing on the object of our attention. Unhealthy relationships are a result of unhealthy beliefs and a habit of attaching our energy to the object. They are habits of where we direct our life force. Cords develop between people that relate in unhealthy ways, thus creating codependent patterns.

To reconcile this once you become aware of an unhealthy relationship, practice the Hara Line Aura Meditation and return to sovereign alignment with the Source Within You. To create permanent change, you can work on identifying and shifting your belief systems that caused the unhealthy patterns, or they will return later until you fully see and heal this part of your subconscious.

Distortion in Our Subtle Bodies

Even before we are born, we begin to absorb the mental patterning of the world beyond our mother's womb. Some people experience trauma within the womb and carry it throughout their life. Additionally, our DNA is filled with energy information from the lifetimes of those who came before us who passed down the genetic coding through our lineages. As mentioned before, life experiences also reactivate stored information in our causal body that brings forth patterns created in past lives.

Traumatic life experiences, memories, and energies often get trapped in all layers of the bodymind complex. Slowly over time, they release so that we do not feel the full brunt of the psychophysical trauma at the moment of the event. When energy is not reconciled, the bodymind tries to release the energy in some way. This can look like crying, sighing, shaking, screaming, sleeping, illness, dreams, and so on. If we practice meditation and self-healing, we can speed up our recovery process significantly.

If we suppress or ignore our emotions and trapped energy, the negative effects begin to show up in our physical bodies. Over time patterns begin to crystallize and become more physical as the bodymind tries to eliminate the distorted energy information. From the most subtle inflammation to the most aggressive cancer, it all has its roots in the subtle energy system. We can use our conscious awareness to reconcile traumatic injuries in our bodies and return to wholeness and vitality.

The *chakras* are constantly broadcasting our internal world and magnetizing events to them that reflect the stored subconscious beliefs. The distortions and trauma stored within our subconscious show up in our life as manifestations of similar circumstances that trigger the trauma patterning. This "clashing" brings our unconscious patterns to the surface so that we can exhaust and potentially integrate the energy information from the past experience and grow in consciousness maturity. From this perspective, we can understand how we create our reality and how everything truly begins within our very own consciousness. As within, so without.

With conscious awareness and subtle energy healing techniques, you can unpack the information stored within the emotions, thought patterns, and physical body events and reconcile the energy. This naturally brings a deeper understanding, and wisdom is revealed through the healing process. This frees up the pathways so that energy can flow freely, and we experience a more joyful, conscious life.

Illness and disease are the body's intelligence giving us a massive wake-up call to tune into our inner being and create a rich, inner life that is luminous and vital. As we tune into subtle energy, we unlock the mysteries of the bodymind's intelligence and begin to accelerate in consciousness growth and authentic empowerment.

Pranayama: Entering the Dimension of Prana

Breathing is one of the main ways that we regulate the movement of the life force in the body. Each inhalation brings in fresh, new life force energy to be used by the body's cells and systems. Each exhalation expels old stagnant energy that is no longer needed by the body. One of the secrets to living a long and vibrant life is the power of conscious breathing.

Breath cycles are made of four stages. *Puraka*, a deep, rich inhalation, focuses the mind and energizes the cells and systems of the body. Inner breath retention, *antar kumbhaka*, equally distributes, calms, and clarifies prana. Conscious exhalation, *rechaka*, releases toxins and calms the bodymind. External breath retention, *bahya kumbhaka*, moves *prana* up the spine to the brain and creates a sense of non-attachment, peace, and inner silence. Women who are pregnant and people with high blood pressure, lung, heart, eye, or ear problems should not hold either phase of breath retention. Instead, they should focus only on the inhalation and exhalations.

Below is a descriptive list of breathing practices, called *pranayama* by the ancient yogis, to get you started with the basics. When you first begin practicing *pranayama*, start with learning to equalize the duration of the inhalation and exhalations in a 1:1 ratio (using a count of four or five seconds) with a slight pause in between inhalation and exhalation. Then increase exhalation duration by doubling the number in a 1:2 ratio. Once this is mastered, add in inhalation breath retention for a ratio of 1:2:2. For more advanced practices, I recommend checking out the *Hatha Yoga Pradipika*.

As you do these practices, keep an easy mind and relaxed body while sitting in a tall, meditative posture. If at any point you feel frustration or tension, stop the practice, return to neutral, and start again when you are ready.

Another practice that I highly recommend is the use of a *neti* pot which looks somewhat like a tea pot and is used for a sinus washing process that clears obstructions out of the nasal passageway. This practice called *jala neti* will increase the body's absorption of prana during breathing and help to awaken subtle consciousness in the brow center.

Three-Part Breathing or Yogic Breathing (Dirga Pranayam)

This breathing style incorporates the full range of breathing capacity utilizing abdominal, thoracic, and clavicular breathing awareness. This practice oxygenates and nourishes the whole body and is great for reducing anxiety and stress.

First, exhale completely until you feel the lower abdomen contract and the pelvic floor lift. Softly release the lower abdomen and allow it to expand with your inhale. After the abdomen expands, allow the chest to expand, feel the energy of the inhale rise up through your spine and into the crown of your head. Softly exhale and reverse the process and allow the air and energy to drain down from the head, softening the chest, exhaling completely until the lower abdomen contracts and the pelvic floor lifts. Repeat, softly extending each segment of the cycle of breath. As you do this, you can imagine that you are surrounded by brilliant, clear, white light. With each breath, you can breathe this fresh light into all the cells of the body.

Samma Vritti: Equal Flow Box Breath

This breathing practice is called "box breath" as the patterning can be thought of as the equal dimensions of a square with inhalation, breath retention after inhalation, exhalation, and breath retention after exhalation. Start simply with a count of four during each stage. Then you can increase the number as you develop control and calmness of the bodymind within each stage. This can be done with regular yogic breathing as well as in alternate nostril breathing.

Kapalbhati: Skull-Cleansing Breath

This breathing practice gets its name because of its revitalizing and healing properties. *Kapalbhati* clears the mind, burns away stagnant energy, clears the respiratory system, and brightens the face and higher chakras. In this practice, inhalations are relaxed, and deep and rapid force is applied to the exhale.

Pregnant or menstruating women should not do this practice nor should people with spinal injuries. If you have high blood pressure, stomach ulcers, or any other health issues, be gentle (one pump per second) until you see how the body works with the practice.

Using the three-part breathing, inhale fully and allow the belly and chest to fill with air. On the exhale, contract the abdomen strongly back towards the spine, feeling a strong pulse of air exit the nose. Softly relax the abdomen and allow the lungs to fill with air. Repeat this pattern, slowly increasing the cycles' speed, creating a rapid breathing pattern that is also relaxed in mind and emotions.

Repeat for around twenty to thirty rounds. On the last exhale, gently push out all the excess air until you feel the pelvic floor and abdomen contract. Drop the chin towards the chest and gently lift the heart towards the chin to make an energetic lock. Hold for a few moments, then release the head and soften the throat, abdomen, and pelvic floor. Find a neutral position of the spine and return to normal conscious breathing and observe your internal experience. If it feels right, you can add consecutive rounds of practice.

Bhastrika: Bellows Breath

Bellows Breath energizes the mind and body, tones the abdominal muscles, and builds the digestive fire. This is a great practice to do if you are feeling tired, confused, or sluggish. It focuses on equal force of inhales and exhales. The practice is often done with arm movement to help with the expansion and contraction of the lungs.

Sit comfortably and find your natural, three-part breathing. After a complete exhale, bring your arms up above your head, spreading the fingers wide as you reach for the sky, and inhale deeply with gentle force. Exhale by strongly contracting the abdomen towards the spine while simultaneously closing the fingers into fists and pulling the elbow down towards the ribs, contracting the muscles of your arms and abdomen fully as you exhale. Inhale deeply to raise the arms back up above the head and repeat the cycle for twenty to thirty rounds. After you exhale, bring the arms down, rest the hands on the legs or ground, and observe your inner experience. If desired, you can repeat the practice.

Bhramari Breath: Bee Breath

Bhramari Breath uses breath and toning of the vocal cords to send vibrations through the throat and skull. The long exhalations assist the autonomic nervous system by inducing a relaxation response through the lengthened exhales. This practice is excellent for anyone who needs to calm the mind and focus their intention.

Sit comfortably in your meditation posture and do several rounds of full yogic breathing. Raise both hands in front of the face with your elbows pointing outwards, in line with the shoulders, with the palms facing you. Close your eyes, gently press the index fingers to the inner corners of the eyes, place the middle fingers on either side of the nose, the ring fingers above the lips, and the little fingers below the mouth. Use the thumbs to gently close the ears.

Another option is to take your hands and rub them together, activating them with light and energy. Bring the hands up to each side of the head, blocking the ears by pressing lightly on the tragus of each ear to close the ear canal. Take the other fingers and lightly touch the brow with the pads of the fingers. Fingers should be spread across the forehead and hairline.

Once your hand position is set you can begin the "bee's breath." At the top of the inhale, begin to make a humming sound with the lips closed. Draw out the sound and play with the pitch of the tones. Feel the vibrations moving throughout your nostrils, sinuses, throat, and brain. Imagine that your hands' vibrations and energy pulsations are breaking apart unhealthy thought patterns and upgrading the neural pathways. Fill the skull and throat with vibrations. Do this for about six rounds. Then drop the mudra and sound and feel the subtle shifts happening along the pathways of energy.

Nadi Shodhanam: Alternate Nostril Breathing

Alternate nostril breathing balances the right and left hemispheres of the brain and the masculine and feminine principles of consciousness, creating a state of calm focus. This practice is especially useful when you feel anxiety or stress. It is a wonderful practice to do before you start anything that needs your full attention and awareness. There are a variety of methods to do alternate nostril breathing. Here is a basic practice:

Take the index and middle fingers of the right hand and lightly touch the center of the brow. You will be using the inside of the ring finger and the pad of the thumb to block and alternate the passage of air through the nostrils. The other hand can be resting on your lap, in jnana mudra, resting on your heart, or in any other comfortable position.

Using the thumb, gently press against the outside of the nose to close the right nostril and exhale completely through the left nostril, gently contracting the lower abdomen and pelvic floor at the bottom of the exhale. Then breathe in through the left nostril as you release the abdominal contraction. Feel the air and energy circulating in the center of the brow under the fingertips. Gently pause at the top without adding tension to the face or upper torso.

Switch nostrils, block the left nostril with the inside of the ring finger, release the thumb off the right nostril, and exhale through the right nostril until you feel the abdomen and pelvic floor contract. Pause for a moment. Then breathe in through the right nostril feeling the air circulate at the brow. Pause again.

Close the right nostril, open the left nostril, and exhale through the left until you feel the abdominal and pelvic floor contractions.

Repeat for at least two to three minutes or longer. Meditate on smoothing out and evening each segment of the breath. A suggestion of ratio would be to start first with a 1:1 ratio, building up to 1:2.

Combined Practice Suggestion:

- 3 rounds kapalbhati (30-50 pulses per round)
- 2 rounds of Bhastrika (30-50 pulses per round)
- 3 complete breaths (natural breathing)
- 3 rounds of nadi shodhanam (2-3 minutes per round)
- 2-3 minutes of bhramari
- Breath awareness
- Meditation

For a shorter practice, you can skip the *bhastrika* breath and keep the cleansing benefits of *kapalbhati.*

Circular Breathing

This breathing practice goes by many names, some of which are trademarked. This type of breathwork involves deep, continuous breathing cycles that highly oxygenate the body and reduce carbon dioxide. This circular breathing pattern is known to help reduce depression, process and integrate trauma, eliminate fears and phobias, and much more. It is known to induce altered states of consciousness and awaken unconscious memory for processing and integration. Many people report having psychedelic-like experiences. It is not recommended to do this practice if you have cardiac or respiratory health issues. Go gentle at first and see how you respond, then you can decide whether to increase or reduce the intensity or duration of the practice. It is recommended to do these practices with a trained facilitator who can guide you through emotional experiences, involuntary muscle spasms, or other powerful experiences. If you are doing this practice alone, go gently and feel it out.

1. Lay down on a flat and comfortable surface. You may wish to cover yourself with a blanket. Keep the head flat on the ground, no pillow, so that the spine stays long and even.
2. Start with a progressive relaxation body scan.
3. Begin the circular breathing pattern with deep inhalations and deep exhalations, no pausing in between. Try to make it seamless.
4. Be careful not to push or strain the body. Back off the edge a bit.
5. Pick up the speed. Do it a little faster than normal but not so fast that the body tenses.
6. It is perfectly normal and common for the face muscles or the hands or feet to contract. Keep breathing through it, nice and gently.
7. If fear or other powerful emotions arise, breathe through them. You can back off the intensity a bit if you wish.
8. Do the practice for about 10-20 minutes. Then relax completely and feel the effects for another 10 minutes or so.

The Microcosmic Orbit

The microcosmic orbit circulates life force throughout the entire system of the body. Sit mindfully and quiet the mind by bringing your awareness to your breath. Bring the tongue to touch the back of the teeth and roof of the mouth to close the "heavenly gate" and gently lift the pelvic floor to close the "earthly gate." This creates an energetic loop that connects the front and back of the body. Breathe mindfully into the pelvis and imagine that the pelvic bowl is filling with white light. As you inhale, sweep the white light towards your sacrum and up your spine, cresting at the top of the head. As you exhale, sweep the white light down the front of your face and body and back to your pelvis. Continue circulating your awareness, breath, and the white light through this orbit until you feel clear, clean, and balanced in your energy. When you are finished, simply return to regular conscious breathing, and observe your Inner Being's sensations.

Pranic Body Summary

We are a bridge between the higher consciousness realms and Earth, existing in an ever-changing matrix of subtle energy. We access this connection through our hara line and personal energy field. As energy information passes through our energy field, it is dispersed to energy vortexes called chakras, transforming the data through our belief center programming, creating emotions. Emotions pulse out a charge of energy that fractals out along the nadis/meridians to create physical body processes and our perception of ourselves and the world around us. We can use the power of our breathing and breath awareness to reconcile our consciousness and return all systems to health and balance. As we raise our vibration and awareness, we move beyond the need for illness and disease as a teacher of karma and move into the perfection of our Divine Blueprint as conscious embodiments of the Breath of Life.

NINE

Postures for Channeling Light

Mudra is a Sanskrit word for energy locks. They are different ways to posture the body to affect the flow of subtle energy. Different traditions have different ways of holding hands to shift subtle energy. If you know any of them and their effects, you can use those when channeling Light. Otherwise, use your intuition. You may have already noticed that the body subconsciously moves the fingers into certain placements at different times throughout the day. This is especially true for those who have studied healing and the Mysteries in other lifetimes. The subconscious remembers the training and guides the body into postures to open the flow of energy and healing.

When we use the power of mudras, we open our body temple instrument to be an oracle for Divine Consciousness. Mudras are keys to unlocking pathways to meet the energy that is being evoked to channel. When we create a mudra and intend to connect with the Light, our biofield and etheric structures rearrange to allow the Divine Frequency Transmission. This sends waves of Light emanating from the entire body temple out into the field.

As we move about the Earth, we can consciously transmit divine frequencies into the field around us. Our bodies are bio-transducers, constantly absorbing energy from the environment and transmuting it through our body systems. As conscious beings, we can support the collective ascension process by channeling divine love into the Earth Reality.

When you consciously tune into Source Energy and the life force of Gaia, you naturally stand tall with an open chest. You beam loving energy through your entire being, bridging Heaven and Earth. You can beam Truth and Oneness out into the world through your gaze and broadcast light from your hands as you breathe consciously.

I will describe some hand *mudra*s and their possible psychospiritual effects. Although each person will experience the power of these hand positions in their own way, I describe specific hand gestures for different mudras. Experiment with the opposite hand as well and discover your own experience with the hand's placements.

Take a few minutes to try each of these hand placements and postures to feel their subtle energy and consciousness effects. If any of them feel uncomfortable or if you notice unpleasant shifts or changes happening after practicing the mudra, stop working with that mudra. A full list of contraindications for each mudra can be found online or in texts dedicated to the various effects of mudras.

Anjali-Gassho: Prayer Hands Mudra

This mudra is made with both palms together in a prayer position with the thumbs touching the Heart Center. This mudra is used by many spiritual and religious cultures around the world and back through antiquity. This mudra unites the right and left sides of the brain and closes our auric field. It connects us with our divinity and to the power of the heart-mind.

Gyan/Jnana Mudra: Knowledge Mudra

This mudra is made by connecting the index and thumb fingertips and extending the middle, ring, and pinky fingers creating the hand symbol of OK. It is also commonly accepted to do it with the tip of the index finger touching the base of the top knuckle of the thumb. This seal is considered the mudra of Knowledge. It focuses the mind on peace, higher intelligence, and wisdom. When the same mudra is made with the palms facing down it is called *chin mudra* (consciousness mudra) and evokes a feeling of groundedness and concentration. Both are excellent for meditation.

Dhyana Mudra: Meditation Mudra

This mudra is made with the right hand holding the left hand. Allow the thumbs to connect to create a triangular circuit of energy. This mudra connects and unifies the body, mind, and soul through the heart field. It charges our central channel and connects us with the prayerful beings and enlightened masters of the Earth and beyond.

Bhairava Mudra: Fierce Mudra

This mudra is made with the left hand resting in the lap while the right hand rests on top. This symbolizes the masculine (right side) resting into the feminine (left side), creating a harmonious feeling (enhances *pingala*). When reversed with the right holding the left, the masculine energy supports the divine feminine energy for awakening and manifestation (enhancing *ida nadi*). It is said to eliminate negative effects of ego and illness.

Varada Mudra: Bestower of Boons Mudra

Associated with the sharing of blessings, mercy, and love, this mudra is made with the right or left hand with the palm facing forward and the fingers pointing down. I typically place this mudra along the right side of my body below the level of my naval. For me, this mudra generates a peaceful, grounding energy that blesses the field around me.

Abhaya Mudra: Courage/Fearlessness Mudra

This mudra is made with the right hand to the side of the body level with the heart. The palm is facing forward with the fingertips pointing toward the heavens. This mudra evokes peace, dispels fear, and welcomes the protection and presence of the Divine.

Abhaya & Varada Mudras: Blessings & Courage

Combine both mudras using the right (upward) and left (downward) hands to bridge the blessed energies of Earth and Sky. Feel the combined energies of grounded peace and the higher frequencies of the higher realms.

Prana Mudra: Life Force Mudra

This mudra is made with the right hand with the pinky, ring finger, and thumb touching. The peace fingers and index and middle fingers are extended upwards and connected. This mudra activates the flow of prana and the root chakra's grounding power, creating a powerful energy transmission.

Prithvi Mudra: Assimilation Mudra

This mudra is made with the right thumb and ring finger touching, with the peace fingers and pinky extended. This "Seal of Life" creates stability by strengthening and healing the physical body. This balances the earth and fire elements of the body and is powerful for healing many ailments.

Ardhapataka Mudra: Half-Flag Mudra

This mudra is made with the thumb, index, and middle fingers extended while the ring and pinky fingers are bent towards the palm. This "sign of benediction" bestows blessings and frees the consciousness of nuisance and disturbance.

Karana Mudra: Purification Mudra

The mudra is made by pressing the pad of the thumb over the nail of the middle finger with the other fingers extended. The ring finger will likely be bent a bit. This mudra "dispels darkness" by clearing obstacles and challenges on the path of awakening and Ascension.

Intent Mudra

This mudra is made by bringing the palms together in a prayer position in front of the solar plexus with wrists touching the solar plexus and the fingers pointing out away from the body. Right thumb crosses over the left to make a circuit. Space between the palms with fingertips touching. This is a wonderful mudra to do whenever you want to cultivate willpower and strength.

Whole Body Transmission

Bring soft tension into your arms and hands and intend for healing energy to flow through them. Tune into your hara line and your loving connection to Source and Gaia. Turn the palms in the direction that you wish to direct the energy.

While you do this, broadcast Love and Light through your Brow Center in the direction of the person, place, or object you hope to illuminate. Feel radiant and filled with Unconditional Love and Unity. Beam undulating waves of love from your heart. Beam dazzling rainbow light from your entire being and completely fill the space with light. Finish with a blessing and dedication, said out loud or internally, "May all beings be free. May all beings know love."

Heart Beacon

Bring your nondominant hand to your heart and intend to connect with your inner Light. Form the other hand in *abhaya mudra* to hold light and shine it into the world around you. If you want the energy to be a higher frequency, have the palm facing outward, in line with the heart or higher, with the fingers pointing upward. For more subtle and grounded heart energy, have the palm down by the side, fingers pointing down towards the Earth in *varada mudra*.

Creative Beacon

Bring your nondominant hand to touch upon your sacral center/lower abdomen/womb space. Feel your connection to Source and Gaia. With the palm pointing outward and fingertips pointing downward or to the side, beam creative and grounding energies into the space. As you create the energies within yourself, they flow out of your field and into the space.

High Calling

Bring the arms up to the heavens to call in Divine Light from Source. Feel your hara line and breathe into it. This is a powerful pose that will generate a powerful feeling.

Earth Field Awakening

Bow down and place your hands upon the Earth to connect to the planetary grid. Slowly begin to stand and use your intention and movement of your arms to raise up frequencies of Light from within the Earth. I often use the imagery of calling up cities of light and illumined beings from Earth's Light realms. Use this connection to make a dance that awakens the radiant energies of Gaia in your awareness.

Spinning Vortex of Light

Imagine that you are connected to Source and Gaia through a bright pillar of clear light. Spin the body in a clockwise rotation with the arms raised out and imagine that you are spreading light in infinite directions. This will naturally clear your auric field and send beautiful light all around you. Come to stillness slowly. Ground down through your legs. Bring one hand to your heart and one hand to your hara and feel the powerful vortex you have created.

If you would like to learn more about the power of the hands for healing, I suggest studying the sections dedicated to the art of the Laying of Hands.

TEN

Planes of Human Consciousness

Inserted into and extending slightly beyond the etheric structuring and life force processes are the layers of "the mind." The human mind is an ever-shifting kaleidoscope of thought patterns involving reception of sensory impressions from the five senses, creation of mental associations of data input, storage and access of memory, intuitive sensory abilities, discriminatory functioning, universal connection, and pure awareness. As sensory information enters through the physical and etheric body, this information is processed through the mind which then stores sensory data and directs the body of action in its engagement with life.

The mind is the link between body and spirit. When the mind is clouded by limiting beliefs, unresolved trauma, and various forms of toxicity that erode our consciousness and vitality, we perceive life in distortion and limitation, disconnecting our physical self from our spiritual self.

Four States of Mind

The ancient yogis described the mind in three states of waking, dreaming, and dreamless consciousness. When we are the Waker, we experience our physical life and its activities. In this state, all the koshas are active and present even if we are not aware of them at all times. When we go about our day-to-day life, we shift through the awareness of our physical body, breathing and vitality, thoughts and sense of I/me, intellectual knowing and insight, and moments of bliss and unity.

When we are the Dreamer in the dreaming state, we lose awareness of our physical body, but the mind continues to modify the breath, process thoughts and emotions, experience intellectual understanding, and sometimes even experience flashes of joy and bliss from our Bliss Sheath. This is a realm of illusion where objects from our waking life are rearranged into dreams. Much learning happens in dreams as subconscious impressions play out to be exhausted and released. Intuitive dreams offer clues and premonitions of what is yet to manifest in waking life. Many people can have lucid, conscious dreams in which they travel to other dimensions within the Subtle Planes, visit with spiritual guides and soul family, and even travel to friendly spacecraft to be updated for their Earth missions.

When we are the Deep Sleeper in deep sleep, the physical, etheric, mental, and higher mind faculties disappear, and we find deep rest in the undisturbed blankness of the Bliss Body. Even though we do not remember what happened, we know something occurred there because when we awaken, we feel rested and refreshed. We did not fade out of existence temporarily. Our True Self enjoyed the untroubled rest of the blankness and bliss of the *anandamaya kosha* with no objects to experience, just pure Consciousness. This is similar to looking at deep space thinking it is darkness. Yet, when a meteor passes through, we see the light bouncing back off the meteor. Light was there, yet we could not see it until there was an object of experience. Pure consciousness always remains. The Light that you are shines eternally.

As we begin to stir awake, we emerge through the layers of the density of our koshas and take on the issues and identifications associated with each layer. We begin to identify with the bodymind and all its roles and functions becoming the Dreamer once more and then the Waker.

There is yet another state of the mind called *turiya*, which is the pure superconsciousness of the True Self. This "supreme equilibrium" is the conscious experience of salvation, liberation, and Godself-Realization. Once a person achieves and continues to maintain this state of enlightenment, they can exist in the Waking State but are aware that it is a superimposition over the True Nature of Reality. There are no more delusions or limiting mental impressions. Even as they walk through this world, their inner focus is completely established upon the Source of their Being, pure Consciousness itself.

Swami Sarvapriyananda gives a great, real-life example of this using the experience of going to a movie theater. As the Observer watches the projected light images of different names and forms upon the screen, the scenes may change but the Observer remains constant. Even if the screen goes black, the Observer, the Witness of the experience, remains. Pure Consciousness is eternally present; we just get caught up in the projected illusion and the changing forms of our perceived reality.

Brainwave States

(Beta, Alpha, Theta, Delta, Gamma)

The activity of the brain can be looked at in terms of vibrational frequency. When the vibrational frequency is high, mental activity is higher. When the brain is in states of rest or deep sleep, the brain's vibrational output is lower.

Beta brainwave states occur when we are awake and alert. This level of brainwave activity is used when we are active in our day and using analytical thinking and problem-solving. These brainwaves are mostly stimulated by our external environment to keep us safe and engaged.

Alpha brainwaves occur when we are relaxed and focused. This is the first level of trance that hypnotists and meditators use to access their subconscious and higher intellect. This state happens when we are physically and mentally relaxed. We begin to enter this brainwave state as soon as we close our eyes. This brainwave state creates the "glossy-eyed stare" of daydreaming and highway hypnosis when we forget driving segments.

Theta brainwave states are created when we are in deep relaxation and have cultivated inner peace. We are in this state when we are in REM sleep and deep hypnotic trance and meditation. This brainwave state gives us access to non-ordinary reality and shamanic experiences.

Delta brainwaves are the slowest brainwaves and are associated with deep, dreamless sleep. In this state, our physical and subtle bodies are in rest, and we enjoy the blankness of deep sleep.

Gamma brainwaves are the highest frequency brainwaves and are associated with high levels of cognitive functioning as all senses work cohesively at this state. Operating with gamma brainwaves gives the perceiver a higher level of unity consciousness, and loving-kindness. Tibetan monks and proficient meditators have higher levels of gamma brainwave activity. This is related to *turiya*, supreme equilibrium, and the blissful, mystical, transcendental states of superconsciousness including *kundalini* awakening, creative genius, flow states, and *samadhi.* These high-consciousness vibrations are generated by inner experiences and spiritual practices that focus awareness on the Self and unification with the Supreme.

Antahkarana: Source of the Mind: Inner Instrument of Being

Antahkarana is the source of the mind, the internal organ, and the cause of thought. The mind can be broken into four functions that work together to create our mental and emotional realm.

Transactional Mind: Manas

This is our everyday thinking mind. It coordinates sensory information before it enters our awareness. The senses include taste, touch, smell, hearing, sight, and our ability to sense subtle information. It is our connection to the external world of physical manifestation and subtle energy. A lot of this data enters our mind without our awareness and is stored in the subconscious. We then take sensory information and data from our subconscious which play out on the screen of our mind. This is where indecisiveness lives as conflicting desires and thoughts are bounced back and forth in the duality of the lower mind.

Subconscious Mind: Chitta

The subconscious mind is our heart-mind that creates our emotional state as energy information is processed through the lenses of past experiences and deeply ingrained impressions and beliefs, *samskaras*, which seem to emerge from the background of our mind. This includes the memory of events from this lifetime and other lifetimes buried in our unconscious mind. This is the data center of our dream state as images from our past are reorganized in dream sequences to exhaust subconscious patterning. Within the storehouse of *chitta* are the root causes of biases, proclivities, illnesses, fears, and other impulses that drive our thoughts and actions.

Ego: Ahamkara: The "I" Maker

This is the egoic faculty of the mind and what most people mean when they say "me" or "I." This faculty gives us the awareness of a sense of "I" and is concerned with self-preservation and keeping the body alive. This faculty is the center of all physical, emotional, mental, and intellectual functioning. The ego is not "bad;" it is only dysfunctional when it is clouded by the distortions in the koshas. As one awakens, one disentangles egoic identity from the physical and subtle bodies' associations, moving the sense of "I-ness" into the higher consciousness planes to realize one's true identity beyond individuality. When one meditates on the phrase "I am that I AM" They turn their lower egoic identity and mind towards their higher consciousness identity.

Intellect: Buddhi

Buddhi is the intuitive, enlightened intelligence, the voice of reason, the intellect. It understands, analyzes, discerns, and decides what is most beneficial for our path. If *manas* is the realm of confusion and indecisiveness, *buddhi* is the realm of clarity and insight. This power of the mind can be experienced as flashes of insight, abstract thoughts, intuitive messaging, and knowledge from beyond this physical life. We will get more into this part of our higher mind capacity when we look at the layers of the Causal Mind and buddhic consciousness.

To understand this internal organ, the *antahkarana*, let us visualize an angry lion coming in our direction. *Manas,* the transactional power of the mind, uses the sensory organs to notice something large is quickly approaching. *Buddhi,* our intellectual mind, understands that it is a lion, and it is angry and is coming to attack something. We may have a flash of a memory from our subconscious memory bank, *chitta*, of someone telling us that lions are dangerous. *Ahamkara*, our ego, adds in that the lion is coming towards "me."

Planes of the Mind

Beyond the physical brain in the *annamaya kosha*, the physical body, the mind can be separated into five subtle planes. All six planes are as follows:
- *Annamaya Kosha*: Physical Brain

Subtle Mind: Lower Mind
- *Kamamaya Kosha*: Conscious Mind: Desire Body
- *Manomaya Kosha*: Subconscious Mind: Mental Body

Superconscious Mind: Causal Mind: Higher Mind
- *Atimanasa Kosha*: Supramental Mind: Intuitive Body
- *Vijnanamaya Kosha*: Subliminal Mind: Intellectual Body
- *Anandamaya Kosha*: Subtle Causal Mind: Bliss Body

The first two layers of the subtle mind, *kamamaya kosha* and *manomaya kosha*, are the standard layers of human mental activity and are developed through the struggles and experiences of physical life. This layer of mind deals with our feelings, emotions, and concrete thought.

The deeper three subplanes can be called the superconscious mind, causal mind, or higher mind. The superconscious mind perceives beyond the material reality into the subtle planes and higher consciousness. These layers begin coming "online" once the involution or spiritual awakening process begins. These layers are more rapidly evolved through spiritual practices, being around others of higher consciousness, and through intense desire for unification with the Supreme. As a human being starts the awakening process, it purifies each kosha and untangles itself from the misidentification with the bodymind, moving the center of awareness progressively deeper and deeper towards the knowledge of the transcendental Self, the Source within.

Kamamaya Kosha: Desire Body: Conscious Mind

At the most superficial level of the mind, we have the layer called the *kamamaya kosha*, the body of desire. Some call this the "emotional body," but not all emotions come from this layer. This layer is called "the crude mind" as it deals with our likes and dislikes, our attractions and repulsions, called *raga* and *dvesha* in Sanskrit. This animalistic level of mind deals with the primitive desires of eating, sleeping, procreating, and action in response to our environment. This plane is where our struggles of morality play out and is the birthplace of physical and psychological addictions. This level is developed by life's struggles and is recalibrated and matured through embodied observance of spiritual ethics.

This is the plane of the human personality which is the coloring of the mind from experiences of one's life. This includes collective conditioning, familial conditioning, social conditioning, past deeds, and impressions from past lives which have been reactivated by current life experiences and environments. As we experience life, we begin to reflect on information as it streams through our senses into the mind and take action based on the information and the conditioning and coloring of past experiences. Since we are ignorant of our True Nature as wholeness, desires arise. When we take action from those desires born from ignorance the consequences can be good or bad. True fulfillment comes from directing our desires towards the Divine and service towards all of Life.

Kamamaya kosha is how we sense and give action through the physical body. As subtle energy information streams in from the external reality, the layer receives the data, generates desires based off the sensory input, and propels the organs of action to materialize those desires. When you feel hesitation to go down a dark alley or rush into the arms of your dear friend you have not seen in a while, it is this layer that holds you back or propels you forward. Before awakening, this layer is run by our false ego and the momentum from past experiences. This layer is purified by focusing your mind and actions towards altruistic actions and higher ethical values such as the *Yamas*, *Niyamas*, and Eight-Fold Noble Path described in Buddhism.

What we feed our conscious mind through perception is stored in the subconscious and eventually overrides our conscious mind creating our external personality. As one begins to correct misidentification with the body and false ego, the next step is to control the conscious mind through purification and awareness. A dedicated aspirant will grow in discernment of what sense experiences they wish to engage in. Does a certain activity support liberation and purification, or does it feed the limited ego, dependency, and cycles of suffering? Do sensory experiences feed the six afflictions of passion, anger, greed, delusion, and attachment, or do the activities nourish and inspire your path of liberation?

Four Instinctual Drives

The desire for the mind to experience physicality gave way to the evolution of sensory organs and a physical form, and this layer governs the four primal desires of the body such as self-preservation, hunger, sleep, and procreation. It is said that all other desires "spring up" from these four sources.

While there is nothing inherently "wrong" with these desires, we can either use them from an animalistic, survival mindset and continue on the path of *samsara,* or we can use each of these four instinctual drives to fuel our awakening and the liberation of ourselves and others from suffering. We can use our drive to eat to acquire food from ethical food sources that are organic to contribute to maintaining the health of our body and the health of Gaia. We can use our sexuality to create deeper bonds and unite with our True Nature. We can dedicate our sleep to continued healing and awakening. We can discern when we are acting from egoic self-preservation, or we can follow our Inner Light to do what is harmonic and serve the good of All.

We are constantly streaming information through the sense organs which tends to be intoxicating for the senses and mind, distracting us from our inner world and True Nature. Anyone can relate to an experience of being distracted by some outer experience that derails us from attaining a goal. Most people habitually focus their awareness on the four instinctual drives and the attainment of sensory pleasure with the error in the perception that happiness comes from something outside of us. This is a never-ending cycle as we are constantly shifting and changing from one experience to the next. Happiness comes from union with our Divine Self. In the fleeting moments where we attain some sensory pleasure, we temporarily relax our mind and endless searching which allows a flash of the joy from our Divine Self to be experienced. Soon after however, that experience fades away and we are back on the hunt for more happiness.

To master the instinctual drives, the spiritual seeker needs to learn to detach from the endless seeking for sensory fulfillment and tune into the fullness of the True Nature. This does not mean that one should never eat or never engage in sexual expression, but that one can use those actions to connect deeply with one's True Self, the true source of joy and fulfillment.

As the practitioner grows in increasing awareness of their True Nature, they become discriminative over what desires to follow to bring higher states of union with their True Nature and clearer focus to achieve their goals. Whatever you do, take your inner Source awareness with you and allow this union to bring joy and satisfaction to every area of your life!

Manomaya Kosha: Mind Processing Center: Subconscious Mind

Inserted deeper into the mind, we have the manomaya kosha, the processing center of our mental functions including information management, philosophical ponderings, computation, and memory. This transactional layer uses the organizing power of *manas* and the storehouse of memory from *chitta* to direct our various processes. This layer of the mind deals with instinctual functions, motor sensory functions, perceptual activities, rational decision making, emotional experiences of pleasure or pain from the conditionings of our past deeds, and regular dreaming. This layer controls the conscious mind and is developed through thinking, remembering, and reacting. It is reconciled with *pranayama* practices, proper diet, development of concentration, sacred mantra repetition, meditation practices, and contemplation on divine knowledge.

What Is Yoga?

"*Yogas chitta vritti nirodhah*" — Divine Union is achieved by calming the mind's fluctuations. This happens as we train our awareness to stay focused on the Absolute Reality, our indwelling Divine Presence. Spiritual growth involves growing awareness of the shifts and changes happening in the subtle realms of our experience. As we transform our deeply ingrained beliefs of duality and separation consciousness with compassion and align with the Absolute Oneness of Life, we ascend from our animal nature to merge with the divine.

The tendencies and habits of the mind (*vasanas*) create ripples and fluctuations (*vrittis*) across our mind. These movements of the mind generate our *karmas* (actions), which generate other habits and tendencies (*vasanas*). Continued habits of action create grooves within our mind and create deeply ingrained habits (*samskaras*).

*Samskara*s are the reactive momenta stored within our mental body from highly charged past experiences that left tracks across our mind. Negative *samskaras* keep us in repetitive cycles of suffering and the need for death and rebirth to continue working out our unhealthy patterns. While some *samskaras* can be pleasureful and intoxicating, it is often the negative *samskaras* that we are most aware of because of the suffering that arises from them. These subconscious mind patterns sit in the background undetectable until activated by some trigger in our experience or when receiving healing.

Samskaras are carried over from one life to another. Whatever work we do not complete in one life is transferred to the next. Mostly, these energies operate in the unconscious parts of our being, casting a spell on our mind and limiting our perception of reality, thus reducing our perceptions of freedom and sovereignty.

Negative *samskaras* can be developed through one intense trauma like experiencing a great cataclysm, being attacked, or from endured suffering such as living in an abusive home. Either way, the patterning is established in the mental field and is reactivated by some stimulus. All negative emotion is the product of reactivated momentum from unprocessed trauma.

We are constantly absorbing information into this data processing body. We should be vigilant in monitoring what we take into our mind. To mature and fortify this body, we should use the alchemical power of mantra to transform our thought waves, pranayama practices to reconcile distortion, take action in life from a place of higher morality, and read sacred scriptures to feed the *manomaya kosha* with higher thought patterning.

When we begin to awaken, we begin to infuse our conditioned mind with Higher Truth and Wisdom. We begin to see our life through the lens of enlightened consciousness (*bodhicitta*). We begin to clear our stagnant energies and limiting belief systems to pursue true liberation (*moksha/nirvana*). You can step out of the Wheel of Karma (*samsara*) and achieve liberation by eliminating the self-defeating tendencies and habits of the mind and adopting higher thoughtform patterning through your connection to your Higher Self and Source.

Emotions: Your Guidance System

Most people are experiencing an average of three emotions at any given time. Emotions are indicators of where we are in our path of creation. Take a moment to scan your emotional realm and notice what unique combination of emotional energies you are experiencing right now. Some have a stronger, more dominant charge, while some emotional energy has a weaker charge in the background.

Emotions are energy information created by thought patterns in the mental planes. When most people speak of their emotions, they are speaking about a set of actions initiated as eruptions in the subconscious mind which emerge in the conscious mind to then be rippled out through etheric pathways into the physical body creating changes in heart rate, breathing, muscular tension, and hormonal fluctuations in the endocrine system (*chakras*).

Emotions want to be felt, integrated, and released. Negative emotions like sadness and grief, when repressed and avoided, can stay with a person for lifetimes if not reconciled and cared for with compassion. Any emotion in excess is out of balance. Even positive emotions like joy, pleasure, and creativity can become ungrounded, chaotic, and intoxicating.

Emotional freedom happens when we learn to release any habits and distractions that keep us from experiencing our emotions fully or block us from the insight that the emotion is pointing us towards. No matter how terrible it feels, each emotion can be experienced directly within the loving presence of conscious awareness.

You are not your thoughts and emotions. You are the awareness that observes the rise and fall of each of these experiences. When we still the mind and integrate the information from our emotions, we settle into the framework that supports all experiences, pure loving awareness.

If you find yourself seeking something outside of yourself that will heal you, fix you, bring you love, success, or anything else that you believe will complete you, I invite you to call off the hunt! What you seek is already within you. Bring your awareness to your breath, calm your mind, focus on your heart center, and see what is already present and alive in the very core of your being.

Five Kleshas: Warring of the Mind

Kleshas, translated as "stains" or "pains," are the veils coloring the mind which keep us from seeing reality and our True Nature clearly. They are wave patterns in our mind that make up our blocks, prejudices, addictive cycles, and limitations that keep us from embracing each moment and living life to the fullest.

One: Ignorance — Avidya

When we know better, we do better. When we become aware of a part of ourselves or life that is not understood correctly or we do not have enough information about, we can seek knowledge and learn. This also includes the "veil of forgetfulness/amnesia" from incarnating on Earth.

Two: Overidentifying with Ego — Asmita

The ego is useful in helping us stay out of danger and make certain choices in our life. The ego "goes with what it knows," and resists change. Our soul desires spiritual growth and expansion. Our ego and our soul can work together to create harmony in our lives and make choices that serve our growth. In this way, our higher nature helps our conditioned mind to untangle itself and perceive clearly.

Three: Desire or Attachment to Pleasure — Raga

Suffering arises from our attempts to control or cling to life circumstances or endlessly fulfill our sensory desires. True fulfillment, true pleasure, happens naturally through alignment with our inner Source.

Four: Avoidance, Aversion — Dvesha

Knee-jerk reactions of rejecting new ideas or experiences come from painful experiences of the past stored within the subconscious. We can bring awareness to our aversion to uncover parts of ourselves that need healing so that we can make choices from a clear mind and fresh vision.

Five: Attachment to Life, Fear of Death — Abhinivesha

The root of fear comes from our fear of physical death and the mortality of our human body. When we root our identity in our soul's eternal nature, we can bravely face life and its circumstances in the pursuit of spiritual growth.

Death

Everyone has a different view of what happens after the death of a human body. Much of our beliefs about death come from religious programming that is based on fear and judgment. Most people fear death, consciously or unconsciously, and spend a lot of energy on the fear of death or aging. Much trauma is carried by people because they do not process the death of loved ones healthily. Religious dogma leaves many questions unanswered, and judgment is placed upon people who seek the truth that is missing from their religious institutions. Part of humanity's healing involves reorienting our relationship with death. To know death, we know the deeper value of life. This is the freedom that comes from knowing of and aligning with the truth of Eternal Life.

Three Dantiens: Centers for Meditation

In the meditative and alchemical practices of ancient Asia, three major subtle energy centers are used for meditation and higher consciousness embodiment called the *dantiens*. These three energy centers relate to the chakra system and can be focused upon, purified, and regenerated to create a clear mind and high level of spiritualized embodiment. Here is a brief description of the *dantiens* and how they relate to cognition and intuition.

Brow Dantien

The brain is made of the right and left hemispheres of the brain which are associated with the conscious mind and the subconscious mind.

The conscious mind is made of everything in our awareness at any given moment. The conscious mind is the part of our mind that is analytical and linear. It is useful for helping us make decisions and plan. It operates on what it can see and measure at the moment. It pulls information from past experiences and projects future outcomes and probabilities based on current and past information. It holds our biases and is in control of keeping the body safe. The conscious mind is the part of us that doubts and connects us to our fears. The conscious mind is associated with our personality because it uses the memories and patterns of the past and the projected future outcomes to create a "now" expression and activity. It is self-preserving and "goes with what it knows."

The subconscious mind can be subdivided into two layers. The top layer of the subconscious deals with recent memories and background thought processes, while the unconscious layer of the mind deals with long forgotten or repressed memories including those of other lifetimes.

This dual-layered subconscious mind records all the sensory input from our life experiences with incredible detail. The subconscious is connected, not only to the records of this life, but it is also etherically connected to the memory bank of our other lifetimes and the ancestral memories stored in our DNA. This side is used for reflection and contemplation and is useful for observation and creativity. Both sides of the brain, the reflective and administrative, the spiritual and human, can learn to work together to create cohesion and flow within the mental patterning.

Heart Dantien

The heart-mind is the compassionate processing region. The heart feels out what is best for all and what choices will usher in our desired spiritual growth. Many cultures point towards the power of the heart as being the seat of the soul. Christ taught that the Kingdom of Heaven, the access gateway that connects us with Higher Light Realms of Creation, is within our very own hearts.

Hara/Lower Dantien

This *dantien* is the most known and can also be called the *hara*, the womb, the soft belly, or the sacral chakra, and is our intuitive processing center, a synthesis of vital, emotional, and mental energy. The hara holds the vital life force energy that we received through our connection to our mother. It expands and contracts in three dimensions as we breathe through our belly. It is said that when we extend the length of our breath, we extend the length of our life. When we breathe through our *hara*, we are grounded in our being. We are connected to our emotions and our creative and sexual vitality when we breathe and feel into our hara.

If we truly desire to be grounded, present, and open to life, we can grow in our awareness of these processing centers. Cultivating dynamic symbiotic awareness in each of these areas simultaneously helps us feel more grounded, present, and open. We can easily make choices that align us with our Higher Path and the Greater Good.

When we are in the states of fear and anxiety, we stop breathing from the hara and the heart, and all our energy rushes into our mind. Our digestive system stops, and all our blood rushes to our arms and legs, ready to fight, freeze, or flee. Since our diaphragm is frozen, our neck muscles begin to lift our ribcage up to make way for air. People who do not breathe with their hara habitually tend to have more anxiety-ridden lives and fear the future. They often have chest, shoulder, and neck tension, as well as headaches. To restore a sense of balance and repose, we can practice belly and heart breathing to restore our physical, mental, and emotional bodies.

Exercise for the Three Dantiens

Hara/Lower Dantien

Close your eyes and bring your hands to your hara with the intention to connect and heal. Lightly touch your womb space (men, you have one too) and gently begin to sense and expand your belly breathing. Notice the four parts of the breath. Inhale, pause, exhale, pause. Smooth out the edges of each stage. Imagine that there is a spark of light in your abdomen. With each breath, this light expands and fills your entire womb/pelvic space.

- On the inhale, think "I am grounded."
- On the exhale, think "Here and now."
- Do this for a few moments until you achieve a calm emotional state.

Heart/Middle Dantien

Bring your hands to your heart center and begin to breathe in and out of your heart and upper chest. Relax the shoulders as you gently breathe in and out of your heart. Imagine a spark of light within the core of your heart and help it grow with each breath.

- On the inhale, think "I am the Love."
- On the exhale, think "I am the Light."

Brow/Upper Dantien

Bring your hands so that one hand cups the back of the head in the occiput and the other hand rests on the forehead. Begin to breathe into the brain and skull. Let it pulsate with life force energy. Imagine a flame in the center of the brain and use your breath to expand the light until you feel it pulsing further than your skin.

- On the inhale, think "I am clarity and peace."
- On the exhale, think "I am present and free."

Bring your hands down to rest on your lap and bring your awareness to all three centers. Breathe in and out of all three until you feel radiant and whole.

Identity Beyond Bodymind

In summary, we are not our desires, thoughts, memories intellectual understanding, or the limited egoic self. We are the pure Consciousness that observes all these experiences of the bodymind. As we continue to align ourselves with our higher purpose and walk our dharmic path, we begin to ascend from the animal nature of our primal instinct and egoic nature and begin to see the events and experiences of our life from a higher perspective. No matter where you are in your life, no matter what you have done in your past, you are worthy of stepping off the wheel of the suffering mind and stepping onto the solid ground of your True Nature and being elevated to a whole new reality of being.

ELEVEN

Superconscious Mind

Going deeper within the mind and permeating the previous layers, we find the layers and functions of the superconscious mind. The superconscious mind is also called the causal mind as it is the consciousness vehicle which causes the string of incarnations and movement of our divine will through the bodymind complex. This layer gives us access to wisdom and knowledge from beyond our everyday thinking minds such as wisdom from our past lives, information from the universal hologram, inner promptings from our higher consciousness identity (oversoul), and wisdom from our spiritual guides and masters. When one hears the "voice of God/Spirit" it is because of this higher mind capacity.

The Superconsciousness itself is the Atman, the pure Consciousness which lends existence to our individual consciousness. When I speak of the superconscious mind, I am speak of the higher mind capacity that is illumined by the Superconsciousness.

According to the occult mystery schools, the causal body contains the blueprint seed forms for our subtle and physical bodies. It is the storehouse of past life impressions, holding the Akashic records of the individual soul and memory from past lives.

As Source comes into individuated form as a singular soul/lightbody to begin a string of incarnations, it first takes on a base layer, sometimes called the auric film. The auric film is made of the purest, subtlest matter and is the storehouse which holds the seed forms for the lower consciousness vehicles, koshas. As one progresses through incarnations the virtues, wisdom, and memory from other incarnations is consolidated and stored in this layer.

As the soul-lightbody moves into the next incarnation, latent patterning from previous lives is reactivated by life experiences and is then expressed through the personality of that incarnation. This includes the suppressed and unprocessed reactions, samskaras, which must be reactivated, expressed, and converted into virtue and wisdom in the following incarnations until full reconciliation and ultimate liberation is achieved.

Causal consciousness, the mind illuminated by enlightened consciousness and soul memory and soul knowledge, deals with abstract, holographic thought and is accessed by refining intellectual capacity, spiritualizing one's mind, and reaching for the divine. This layer is slowly activated through one's incarnation. While the lower activities of *kamamaya kosha* and *manomaya kosha* deal with details and concrete linear thinking, causal consciousness deals with essence and holographic intelligence, giving rise to higher intellectual capacity. When one receives "downloads" it is experienced as a flash of holographic information that is slowly unpacked and integrated.

This higher mind structuring is the arena for rapid spiritual evolution. A person who uses the superconscious mind makes a habit of withdrawing their senses through meditative awareness and contemplation to feed an inner philosophical discussion in an attempt to understand the cause behind all things. The superconscious mind gives us the ability to witness life as an observer, a witness to the mind, energy, and material world. It is a higher mental body that is not directly engaged in moment-to-moment life but is rather acutely aware and quietly infuses the lower mind processes with higher knowledge, flashes of insight (aha moments), and wisdom. Beyond the superconscious mind is the pure Awareness shining from the Divine Self, which illumines all experiences of the bodymind and external reality.

The superconscious mind is where we begin to experience awakened intelligence, *buddhi*, and the ability to discern and grow spiritually through meditation, reflection, and self-study. *Buddhi* is the vehicle for our Inner Source and the conduit for divine knowledge to reach our mind and give action through the physical form.

The causal mind or superconscious mind is the seat of our spiritual morality that moves us out of animal nature and into ethical, spiritually informed thoughts and actions. It satiates the hunger for sensory intoxication and replaces it with the ability to surrender to higher willpower and grow spiritually. This is the place in our being that fuels our growing capacity to be in Service to All of Life. The superconscious mind gives us the power of divine conscience, discernment, discretion, deep knowing, and intuitive feeling. Establishing our awareness of this level of our being moves us out of the darkness of ignorance into the ascension of consciousness.

When we have purified the physical, etheric, and lower mental layers, we begin to establish ourselves in the Higher Mind and our awakened buddhic intelligence. We access this *kosha* through mindfulness, meditation, intelligent self-care that is heart/self-love focused, reading sacred texts, traveling to new places, being around others of higher consciousness, and direct self-inquiry into the true nature of our being.

In Advaita Vedanta, they call these layers the *vijnanamaya kosha and the anandamaya kosha.* In another philosophy, these *koshas* are separated into a three-layered system with each layer having distinct functions that contribute to the qualities of that sheath. The layers of the superconscious mind are as follows:

- Intuitive Layer: *atimanasa kosha*
- Intellectual Layer: *vijnanamaya kosha*
- Bliss Layer: *anandamaya kosha or hyranyamaya kosha*

As we start to turn our focus inward to the subtle parts of our mind, we begin to discover a "still small voice", spiritual consciousness, that begins to lead our lives into higher expressions of nobility, devotion, and intuitive genius. As our higher psychic sensitivities activate, we begin to work with the powers of the universe to manifest higher outcomes for our life and move out of linear, finite consciousness into quantum cosmic consciousness. We begin to cultivate laser-sharp focus and the ability to discern what is right and good for the highest benefit of All and act from a place of selfless service and compassion. We begin to move from standard evolution to a higher order of spiritual involution to realize ourselves as Source in Form, moving from mundane human life into multidimensional superconsciousness. Now we will go through each kosha of the superconscious mind to understand how it is developed and the qualities of consciousness it provides.

Atimanasa Kosha: Supramental Mind: Intuitive Layer

The most superficial layer of the superconscious mind is what is called the intuitive layer or the *atimanasa kosha*. In the Vedic systems, this layer's functions are considered to be the *vijnanamaya kosha*. This supramental mind is beyond the comprehensibility of the average human mind. This is the level of the mind which begins to shine with the desire for spiritual awakening as our mundane human mind begins to contact the Cosmic Mind and ascend towards superconsciousness. Accessing this layer moves us out of the experience of linear time and into nonlinear time giving us access to information from past, present, and future.

This is said to be the layer where *samskaras* are stored and reactivated to be experienced through the *manomaya kosha* acted upon though the *kamamaya kosha* and physical form. As the mind clashes with itself, a process starts that awakens higher understanding and perception and begins to move the processes of the mind beyond normal human experience. We access this layer when we are in states of contemplation or in our creative "flow state." This layer gives birth to the creative genius, flashes of insight, and serendipitous discovery. When the lower mind is confused and hindered, this layer disseminates flashes of insight birthed from an understanding of past, present, and future events.

This is the arena for all paranormal and psychic phenomena of the mind. This psychic layer gives us access to extrasensory perception and psychic gifts such as telekinesis, telethought communication, precognition, intuitive message dreams, inner prompting through synchronicity, and the *"clairs."* Activation of this supramental capacity is stimulated and enhanced by being around others who are psychically activated and of higher spiritualized embodiment. Supramental activation happens when we travel to new environments and through spiritual education.

The Clairs: Intuitive Psychic Senses

The descent of *buddhi* from the higher planes into our consciousness is described by the Christians as the white dove of the Holy Spirit descending upon the believer to activate spiritual awakening and the Gifts of the Holy Spirit. The Gifts of the Holy Spirit include our extrasensory perception capacities, our spiritual gifts, and the ways the Divine Will moves through us to inspire enlightenment in the world.

The development of psychic gifts, or *siddhis,* is a natural occurrence that happens as we go through the involution and activation process of Ascension. As the samskaras are exhausted, our extrasensory perception increases, and we are able to access our spiritual gifts and receive intuitive messages from our Higher Self and spiritual guidance team with greater precision and clarity. Our vessel needs to be cleared of distortions in the physical, etheric, and lower mental bodies to give us the ability to discern what comes from the conditionings of the mind and lower egoic identity structure and what impressions come from enlightened and divinely influenced sources.

When we begin to awaken, we become increasingly more energy-sensitive as we tune into the subtle parts of our experience through our Inner Being. We move beyond the typical five senses and begin to expand and incorporate our intuitive and empathetic senses.

While most people are aware of the standard five senses, many have developed extrasensory perception and have become multisensory as described in *The Seat of the Soul* by Gary Zukav. Everyone on the planet is evolving to multisensory perception as an expanded empathetic nervous system comes online as the superconscious mind capacity activates in humanity.

Highly sensitive people, sometimes called empaths, have developed a range of senses that exceeds the standard sensory perception. These people have an acute ability to notice, sense, and feel shifts in energetic frequency, sound, and other people's emotions, thoughts, and intentions. Due to their sensitivity to stimulation, many "empaths" isolate and develop phobias around social situations. Energetic hygiene practices and learning to work with one's own light power can build resiliency so that highly sensitive empaths can stay grounded, centered, and clear in their own energetic boundaries.

In the early years of life, we may have been "more open" and in tune with our empathetic and intuitive senses but over time learned to dull our perceptive abilities because of conditioned belief systems and toxins in our food and environment (e.g., fluoride), or we may have "dimmed our light" for emotional safety and to blend in with our family and mainstream culture.

These extrasensory abilities give us access to the unified quantum field, allowing us to "download" information from the information matrix. This allows us to receive information telepathically from other people and beings that are local and nonlocal. Our third eye allows us to project our awareness into other times, places, and dimensions. We can also use this natural psychic intelligence to receive information about future events so that we can navigate timeline probabilities and adjust our intentions and actions to manifest the desired outcome. While someone is talking to us, we can also be aware of what emotional and mental projections they are broadcasting simultaneously, so that we can interact from a place of deeper understanding.

We can use this system as an "upload" technology to project our highest visions and intentions to allow the hologram of reality to materialize our inner dream into reality. This naturally happens when someone prays for truth and healing. This communication system will connect ascending humanity through heart-resonant telepathic communication as we move into New Earth. Many are already experiencing an increase in psychic communication and extrasensory perception.

Psychic intuitive abilities are our natural birthright. As we awaken spiritually and detoxify all of our systems, these senses become sharper and more pronounced. Everyone has these abilities. Soon, everyone on the Earth will have them activated and online fully at a level that we cannot even imagine from our current level of understanding. These intuitive abilities are often referred to as the "*clairs*," which derives from French and means "clear." As a prefix to one of the senses, it conveys a super-sensory extension or the ability to gain insight beyond the range of ordinary, physical perception.

Below is a list of the basic intuitive senses and a general connection to the individual learning styles: visual, auditory, verbal, physical, logical, social, and solitary. Your primary and secondary learning styles are most likely your primary and secondary intuitive senses.

Commonly Known Intuitive Senses

1. **Clairsentience:** Clear physical feeling is the ability to receive subtle information from the world around you. This includes sensing the past, present, and future energies of people, places, and objects. Can be connected to kinesthetic learning

2. **Clairempathy:** Clear emotional feeling is the ability to sense and feel the emotions, thoughts, and physical sensations of another being in your own body. Can be connected to social learning and kinesthetic learning.

3. **Claircognizance:** Clear knowing is the ability to know information intuitively without having it physically manifested. This information is downloaded from our Higher Self, who has a higher, broader perspective. Can be connected to self-enquiry and solitary learning.

4. **Clairaudience:** Clear hearing is the ability to hear messages from

your Higher Self or spirit beings. This includes hearing the thoughts of other people. Can be connected to aural/auditory learning.

5. **Clairvoyance:** Clear sight is the ability to perceive information through internal imagery. Can be connected to visual learning.

6. **Clairesalience:** Clear smelling is the ability to intuit information through the sense of smell.

7. **Clairgustance:** Clear tasting is the ability to receive intuitive information through the sense of taste.

8. **Clear Channeling:** Mediumship, or spirit channeling, is the ability to communicate with nonphysical beings and consciousness structures. This can include souls who have passed beyond the veil of physical life or beings that exist in other dimensions. Can be connected to verbal learning.

Astral Realm Precautions

When we use our intuitive abilities, it is important to process the information through the light of our heart and higher consciousness. Information from high sources is always loving and patient. The Astral Plane is a parallel plane to our physical universe consisting of subtle energy, desire, emotions, and nonphysical beings. We explore this plane each night in our astral body, the consciousness body of our mind. There are many wonderful astral beings of light but there are also nefarious beings and pervasive energies on the lower parts of the Astral Plane.

Some people who say they channel higher consciousness beings are channeling lower astral beings who feed off low vibrational emotions such as fear and confusion. If someone claims to channel ascended beings or some collective star nation, be sure to check and feel their energy and vibration to see if they are truly a pure conduit. Information coming from high consciousness beings will always be empowering and uplifting.

Use your heart and body to discern what information inspires love and what information causes contraction and fear. Many empaths are tortured by psychic attacks because they have not developed a powerful light quotient in their field, do not practice proper energetic hygiene, and have not learned how to discern energy through their heart and higher consciousness. While everyone has a "teacher that lives within," I always suggest that people find a professional guide and quality education as they explore new frontiers of their psychic capacity.

Everyone who is awakening is beginning to open these spiritual senses. Eventually, everyone on the Earth will be masters at these abilities and much more! They are the natural birthright of any human being, and everyone will develop them at their own pace and at the appropriate time.

Try not to compare yourself with others. For some, they are "scheduled" to open their gifts later than others so that they can stay focused on the task at hand. If we were all highly empathic psychic channels, we would likely be distracted from doing some of the more mundane daily tasks that are important for our missions.

We should also be careful of the spiritual ego that tries to attain these gifts for power or to make us feel valuable. Continue cleaning the body, working with prana and breath, and feeding and training the mind with divine knowledge. Practice! Practice! Practice! All is coming!

Vijnanamaya Kosha: Subliminal Mind: Intellectual Layer

Going a bit deeper, we have the Intellectual Layer, the *vijnanamaya kosha*. This "special knowledge" sheath gives us the feeling of sentience and the ability to discern what is truth and what is an illusion. This is the layer that helps us be "in the world but not of it". It gives us the power to be unattached to sensory experiences and see life events from the perspective of the Observer, keeping us from being entangled in the psycho-emotional polarities.

This is the layer of the reflected consciousness of Source in each human. This reflected consciousness creates the sense of an individual self by capturing the Light of Pure Consciousness and reflecting it upon the ego, the sense of "I". The "I sense" then illumines the rest of the mind. From this the body and sense organs get consciousness and start functioning. The body borrows awareness from the sense organs. The sense organs borrow awareness from the mind. The mind borrows awareness from the reflected consciousness. The reflected consciousness borrows awareness from the Witness Consciousness, the Pure Light of Consciousness. We mistakenly think the body or mind is conscious, yet all borrows existence and sentience from the Light of the True Self.

To understand this, we can think of when a person looks into a mirror and sees their reflection. The person is the True Self, the mirror is the reflected consciousness, and the reflection is the ego, the limited self. This is how the Intellect and Ego, the mirror and reflected image, merge to create the individual self via the power of the Witness, the pure Consciousness which you are.

Imagine a garden filled with different shaped buckets of water all around the garden. The one sun shines and is reflected in each bucket creating individual reflections. The conditions of the water in each bucket are different. Some are pure water, some are muddy, some are disturbed and rippling. Yet the one sun shines in all. From this example, the buckets are our unique bodies, the conditions of the water symbolize the conditions and contents of our mind. Yet one Light of Consciousness shines through all.

We use the reflected consciousness to observe and experience the conditions of the world and our bodymind. The problem is that ego gets entangled with the bodymind and not the true Source of the reflection, the pure Consciousness which we truly are. In meditation, we use this reflected consciousness to turn inward towards the True Self, the One Light which illumines all.

The "wisdom" or "special knowledge" from this layer is not typical worldly knowledge but wisdom that comes from our True Self giving the individual direct cognition, clear knowing, pure intelligence, and higher understanding.

Access to this layer gives us the ability to be nondual in this world of duality. This layer gives us the power of *viveka*, the power of discrimination and discernment of what is right or wrong for our being and what is illusion versus what is of the Absolute. This is the seat of *vairagya*, or non-attachment to and dispassion for worldly pleasures and sense gratification. This layer gives us the higher consciousness qualities of patience, one-pointedness, serenity, humility, grace, and intrinsic nobility.

This sheath is developed through psychic clashing, practices of concentration and meditation, as well as the study of sacred texts and philosophies. These practices activate one's inner wisdom and develop the powers of discernment and dispassion for worldly pleasures so that one can source joy and fulfillment from one's True Nature. Tune in. Turn on. All you seek is found within!

TWELVE

Bliss Body and Unity Consciousness

Going a bit deeper in the superconscious mind we discover the *anandamaya kosha*, the Bliss Body. I have read of this layer being called the *hyranyamaya* kosha, the Golden Sheath because of the golden radiance that shines from one who accesses this layer. It can also be called the Buddhic Body or Spiritual Body as it is the layer that shines with awakened spiritualized intelligence.

The function of this layer is to fuel the desire for limitlessness and catalyze devotion towards the Divine in All and to inspire yearning for unification with the Supreme. This layer expresses itself through buddhic consciousness or what many call unity consciousness giving us access to the highest levels of love, unity, charity, and sympathy.

This layer is considered *avidya*, ignorance, because it is the veil of *maya* that is first projected from pure Consciousness to begin creating the experience of a limited being. Yet ignorance is bliss as some of the Light from our True Nature shines through this veil to create the other layers of our bodymind. We transcend this layer as we gain knowledge of the transcendental Self.

This is the most evolved layer of the mind giving us the highest experiences of joy, serenity, contentment, love, and peace. This layer gives us access to the spaciousness and emptiness of mind and pure bliss. If the Intellectual Layer witnesses the experience of bliss, this layer gives us the experience that we ARE the bliss.

This part of our being is felt as completeness, wholeness, and fullness and is anchored into our awareness after long practices of concentration and meditation on the luminous bliss of our True Nature. When we experience flashes of bliss, unity, and joy in our waking life, it is because we have tapped into this layer of our consciousness.

When we access these states of being, we bridge ourselves with the unity of Creation and become active, organic extensions of the grace and benevolence of Source. When we are in these states, we are deeply nourished, our cup runneth over, and we emanate the redemptive power of Source Consciousness.

As an awakening individual progresses step-by-step through the subplanes of this level, incrementally realizing higher and higher levels of unity consciousness, a point is reached where the individual no longer sees other people as separate but experiences the "other" as himself or herself in another form. This is beyond understanding this concept as "theory" but truly being aware that all individuals are our True Self looking out through different forms. As one's conscious awareness grows wider and wider, this love extends out to all of humanity and all levels of Life, whether good or evil, as they are all reflections of the Oneself.

At this level of the superconscious mind, we are accessing divine knowledge, divine wisdom, and divine intuition as we begin to push the upper limits of our awareness to perceive the transcendental Self. In the intellectual intuition of the *atimanasa kosha* and *vijnanamaya kosha*, we perceive information about external events through psychic impressions and direct knowing. In buddhic intuition, we can empathetically FEEL the information within our own conscious awareness as if we were that being or circumstance.

When this level is developed, the aspirant has established their mind in the awareness that there is no separate self, yet one's individuality is one with All. The aspirant has thus released all doubts and uncertainties regarding the spiritual impermanence of existence because of dedicated self-study and through an embodied understanding of Universal Law. At this level, the aspirant has dissolved all superstitious beliefs and egoic desires for sensory fulfillment so that one's will is clear and determined and is engrossed in higher wisdom and higher love. At this stage, the aspirant knows that there is no path above any other and that all paths lead to the same realization of Unification.

This part of our being is undiscovered and underdeveloped in most of humanity. Most do not know this state of beingness is possible because they have not quieted and purified their mind enough to listen to the deeper part of themselves. Maybe they are distracted by physicality and endlessly look for happiness "out there." Maybe they believe themselves to be impure and would never dare think that such divine bliss lives within them. Yet those who are brave enough to face their shadow and take the inward journey are most blessed to discover complete liberation, freedom, and the truth of their immortality.

Samadhi and the Development of Liberated Consciousness

We access our Bliss Body when we are in acts of selfless service (*seva*), acts of devotion (*bhakti*), and the joyful calmness of mind focused on the Divine (*samadhi*). We access this state in deep sleep or states of untroubled rest. In this state, we are completely absorbed in the eternal unfolding of perfection of the NOW.

In *samadhi*, we rest in blissfulness with no attachments, no desires. We are untethered from the pull of "the world" and are absorbed in the luminosity of our True Nature, shining our golden radiance into the world. We naturally enter this state at night when we rest in the blankness of sleep and awaken feeling refreshed and rejuvenated. Yet the true practice is to enter this place of unification and revitalization while in the waking state.

The general concept of *samadhi* is that the practitioner begins to be able to unify their mind with the higher consciousness reality more and more consistently until full and lasting liberation and unification are attained. There are different steps and stages of *samadhi* described in different philosophical traditions. Some are states of unification with objects outside of one's individual self, and conversely, there are states of *samadhi* achieved by turning one's awareness inward towards the *Atman*, the Source Consciousness within.

The experience of divine bliss of the Buddhic Body comes from dissolving concepts of separateness and surrendering the limits of intellectual understanding. From this place, all that is left is the desire for unification with the Supreme. This reaching of one's awareness towards the Divine then begins to open a level of liberation that is only found by transcending even the bliss consciousness to the nirvanic consciousness of your True Self.

The Bliss Layer gives us the brilliant radiance of our unhindered I AM presence. When one establishes their center of consciousness from this plane, the lower ego has completely dissolved at this final stage before complete unification with the Supreme. This merging with the Light while maintaining the "I AM Consciousness" presence is the last station before full realization.

As the Initiate continues to amplify this desire and devotion, the I AM experience fades away and all that is left to experience is the continual experience of Light. A being with this level of consciousness could be called a *jivanmukta*, a liberated being who shines with the brilliant light of true joy and true bliss. These liberated beings walk through life's day-to-day activities while maintaining this golden radiance of higher consciousness. This level of enlightenment is called an *asekha* in Buddhism, a "non-learner" who has realized and maintains nirvanic consciousness while being in physical form to bring the higher dimensional plane to the physical plane to assist others in their evolution.

Beyond this phase exists the state of consciousness that goes by many names in many traditions. This highest state of unification and absorption can be called *kaivalya*, or *nirvana* as it is called in Buddhism, *moksha* in the Vedic traditions, and the "salvation" that the gnostic Christian teachings speak of. In this state, there is complete absorption in the Absolute as the individual mind has completely dissolved, merging Subject and Object as One in radiant nondual consciousness.

As one progresses through this final station all desires are dissolved including the desire for unification with the Supreme as one progressively realizes they have always been that One Light of Consciousness. At this level of enlightenment, the Seeker has released all egoic identity, all samskaras, all distorted limiting belief structures, all efforts of the mind, and crosses permanently into the liberated nondual consciousness of the True Self. Once one pierces into this plane, they have moved into a level of consciousness that is inconceivable to the average human mind that only knows life through the experience of the senses and limited egoic identity structure.

When one achieves this state of liberated consciousness, they have achieved the state of Ascended Masters, beings who have perfected their consciousness with divine bliss, divine wisdom, and divine power and live as immortal intelligence. These beings have no need to take on a physical form for developing consciousness and only come to Earth on "mission-related" incarnations to assist collective human awakening.

You Hold the Keys to Heaven

Most people spend their entire life slaving away and wasting their life force to build an empire to enjoy during retirement. They then spend all of their retirement using their acquired resources to repair their body and mind that they damaged by trying to build external wealth and external power. True happiness cannot be bought, hoarded, or acquired through the physical world. Even if we have immeasurable talent, youthfulness, wealth, health, and intelligence, there is still a greater state of fulfillment and joy that can be experienced here and now through union with your True Nature.

You do not have to wait until you die to receive salvation or liberation from cycles of suffering. The doorway to the Kingdom of Heaven is within your very heart right now and you hold the keys to unlock your blissful inheritance. If you can detach from the drives of the body and the desires of the mind that obscure your bliss, you can awaken to the God Force that lives within you. You can detach from the endless seeking of sensory attainment, walk the path of devotion, and claim the benefits of Heaven in this very life.

You do not have to be a renunciate to do this, you can align with your inner teacher, your inner monk, and make Ascension and God-realization your sole purpose in life. In each moment you can choose to release intentions that protect your egoic identity and align with Unconditional Love and Service to All.

Every act in your life can be of reverence and devotion which moves you from seeking worldliness to spiritual seeking, to the attainment of true and lasting peace and liberation. This is the blessing promised to the God/Higher Love-seeking souls of this generation, to finally step off this wheel of suffering and claim our divine inheritance as Children of God. Let us fully awaken as Source itself, right here, right now, forever and ever!

THIRTEEN

5D New Earth Consciousness

Some believe that *samadhi* is the final stage of awakening. There are other levels of ascension beyond what is currently experienced on the planet. Yeshua ben Joseph, Jesus of Nazareth, demonstrated this after the resurrection when he appeared to his closest disciples in his Fourth Density Lightbody form. This is the same form we all will be developing into as we transition into New Earth with renewed bodies with 5D+ consciousness or what has been coined as christ consciousness.

Jesus exemplified and publicly demonstrated what the sages and mystics have practiced in secret caves, monasteries, and hidden orders throughout time. He followed his spiritual path, his *dharma*, to the end and beyond. Even while nailed to the cross, he KNEW that the truth of who he is exists beyond the physical, etheric, mental, intellectual, and bliss bodies.

Our True Nature as God can be described as "*Satchitananda:*"

- *Sat:* Eternal Existence or Eternal Truth
- *Chit:* Eternal Light of Consciousness
- *Ananda:* Eternal Bliss

Or in the words of Christ, "I am the Way, the Truth, and the Life!" This means he realized himself as that One Light of Consciousness, the nondual Source of Creation. We are all that One Light of Consciousness. Part of his mission was to publicly demonstrate the path we all can take and the level of ascendency we all can attain.

I have had a somnambulistic client who channels all the consciousness levels in her legacy with perfect clarity. When we are working together, her oversoul completely merges with her body and shares profound information about all the client's many lifetimes and has access to many higher consciousness beings. When her oversoul does not have an answer, her oversoul says "Let me shift up to the monadic level to see if there is information there." Then I speak with that part. She has shifted even higher to a 16th-dimensional archangelic aspect of her that is harder for her body to channel because the frequency is so high and the information is abstract, more like light geometry than actual decipherable messaging. In The Book of Knowledge: The Keys of Enoch J.J. Hurtak describes the higher aspects as the oversoul, christed oversoul, and elohistic oversoul. Even further beyond that is the pure Source Consciousness, our true point of origin, our True Self.

We are eternal, existing beyond time and space. We are the pure Light of Consciousness that illuminates the Cosmos. We are the Absolute Bliss of Source experiencing itself in myriad forms in an eternal dance of Ascension and Descension, forgetting and remembering the Truth of Eternal Life and Eternal Love and Oneness.

When we are in the dance of life, we are not the physical body, the skin, the muscles, the bones, and the blood in motion. We are not the breath and life force that power the rhythmic flow of our body's movement. We are not the thought process that guides the body into rhythm and flow. We are not the sense of feeling that "I am dancing." We are not even the joy of being lost in the dance. We are the nondual Consciousness that experiences all of these names and forms arising, abiding, and dissolving in the light of our awareness.

As we travel through our different koshas in search of our True Self, we discover that there is no object of Self to be found and that our true identity is paradoxically transcendental and imminent. What has seemed hidden from us has in actuality always been present. We are all-pervading, ever-existent, and eternally free! This illuminates the power of the Hebrew mantra "Ehyeh Asher Ehyeh." — "I AM THAT I AM." The use of this powerful statement acknowledges the ability for the individual identity to be absorbed into the divine identity. It immediately connects us to the Higher Consciousness Reality and the power of Ascension.

Bring your hands to prayer position at the heart and sing the mantra repeatedly, in Hebrew or English, with focus, devotion, and praise. Let the reverberations echo through your being to dissolve all that no longer serves you. Keep singing it until you are absorbed in the vibrations of Eternal Existence, Eternal Consciousness, and Eternal Bliss!

You are the Ocean of Consciousness. Pure infinite existence itself. Let the waves rise and fall. Entire universes arise, exist, and dissolve within you, the One Light of Consciousness. Let karma do as it may. Let old age come, let disease come, let poverty come, let death come, let ill fame come. You lose nothing by it. All exists within you, the One Light of Consciousness. What has been, what will come, is nothing compared to the fullness you are here and now!

Test Run of the New Human Template

On February 24, 2017, I experienced a rapturous, transformational experience that completely shifted my perception of reality. I was downloaded with a higher coding and was blessed to experience a "test run" of humanity's next embodiment. I was transported psychically to a higher dimension, where I met with a council of radiant Elders who began to place a new holographic overlay on top of my current subtle operating system. My sacral center was updated and expanded (possibly to a fifty-foot radius or more), and I was told that I would use this energy field to attract others. Two golden chakras formed above my shoulders, and codes of Light from foreign languages flowed all around me. The codes were strange letters and symbols, Light language "fire letters," that I assume are from a higher vibratory alphabet.

Not only were they illuminated as I watched them sparkle and shine around me, but I could tell they each had sentience. I had a distinct feeling that I was in a "*merkaba*" even though I did not know what that was at the time. A *merkaba* is a Divine Light Vehicle used by higher dimensional Beings of Light and Ascended Masters to travel throughout Creation. We all will have access to our own individual *merkaba* field as we shift into the New Human Template and 5D consciousness.

When I was brought back into my body and became aware of where I was on the Earth again, I felt merged with all of Creation. I felt one with the air around my body. I felt that not only did I experience the breath and movement of the Universe, but I had a clear knowing and feeling that I WAS the Universe breathing and moving. Powerful feelings of life force and magnetism pulsed from the core of my being. The stars throbbed love and sentience. It was as if I was seeing stars for the first time. It was as if each star was a unique being witnessing my transformation with great joy and compassion.

As I walked around the forest, I felt that I was intimately intertwined with the consciousness of Nature and all of her kingdoms and that I could control the elemental forces at will. This was a bit concerning for me as I realized the immense responsibility that comes with such power. I felt that I was not limited to one time and space and that, if I wanted to, I could project myself where I willed myself to be.

As I was walking, different Elders and higher consciousness forms moved in and out of my psychic awareness sharing information and perspective with me about my future and role on the planet. A fearful thought rippled through my energy field as I feared that I was insane or arrogant for believing this experience. This caused me to noticeably drop in confidence and life force. I immediately heard that I was "just not used to this level of embodiment in this life. Get used to it!" and was immediately recharged with energy. I was psychically aware of a large, cloaked spacecraft docking close to where I was. I felt I had a deeply personal relationship with that ship, and that the beings on the ship were witnessing and conducting this rapid, evolutionary embodiment process.

I found a place to lay down on the ground as "They" performed multidimensional psychic surgery on all my layers and bodies, completely recalibrating my cellular structure. I had a feeling that "old me" was leaving and that a newer, wiser aspect of my consciousness "walked in" and was being downloaded and integrated into my body.

This went on for several hours. Eventually, I went to bed and woke up twenty hours later. I was extremely dehydrated and quickly chugged about a gallon of water. At this point, the effects of the upgrade had integrated and receded into the background to be reactivated in the future at the appropriate time.

This experience catapulted me forward on my path of awakening. Since that experience, I have a much higher spiritual station that is my default consciousness mode. I have had a few other situations similar to this one that I have mentioned previously in this book where further updating has been done on my body's organic technology and my consciousness.

One of the reasons I had this experience is so I could share it with humanity to let them know that major cellular and consciousness transformation is coming that is beyond having a more positive approach to life (regular awakening). Many people acknowledge spiritual awakening but do not fully grasp or accept the truth of the rapid planetary and human biological transformation happening NOW.

Many people think that the "New Earth" is simply humanity learning how to get along where everyone is polite, vegan, and recycles trash. There is MUCH MORE! The New Earth is a completely new light spectrum reality where we exist in perfected, restructured, and upgraded bodies of Light with a fifth-dimensional and above consciousness anchored in multidimensional unity consciousness. This will be true for every single person left on the planet as she shifts. This is available to all people regardless of sex, gender expression, genetic lineage, socioeconomic status, political affiliation, and so on. This is for ALL SOULS — every member of our human family who has opened their heart to Higher Love.

We cannot even comprehend the world we are about to inherit. Miraculous reality will be our moment-to-moment experience. Our bodies will no longer have diseases because we will be in a vibration beyond disease. We will have multidimensional communication abilities with the higher realms. We will be physically present on the Earth while simultaneously projecting our conscious awareness into the higher light dimensions. Our bodies will be avatars for the Overself meaning we will be more of a collective of souls than one individual identity. Supersonic human life is coming, and it is ours for the claiming!

Charge to the People of Light

So, this is it. This is our opportunity to shed every single whisper of shadow and rise up into our greatness and Light. While grieving is inherently intertwined in this global transformation process, it is also time for celebration for making it to this Grand Transformation of Life. Every step is part of our victory march as we finalize what all of us have been working towards for many, many lifetimes. There is no stopping the avalanche of Light that is coming!

This is the last temper tantrum of humanity. These are the last wars, the last of illness and disease, the last of oppression, the last of murder and human trafficking, the last of the crimes against children and the Earth, the last of all of the muck that humanity has been slinging back and forth for thousands of years! This is the completion of an eternity's worth of karma for all who are ascending!

We are the generation that finally puts an end to this madness. We are the builders of a New Earth awakening to our own Christhood, Buddhahood, and Krishna Consciousness. Doesn't it feel GREAT TO CLAIM THIS IN OUR KNOWING?!!

- Let us release fear and lack consciousness so that we may receive the full bounty of our divine birthright as beloved Children of Earth and Heaven.

- Let us release our egoic identity and come into the right relationship and connection with all of Life as Divine Creators in form.

- Let us put aside our service-to-self compulsions and rest in the Divine Will as pioneers of consciousness and leaders of the New Earth!

- Let us use the redemptive power of forgiveness and open our hearts with loving-kindness, compassion, equanimity, and empathetic joy as reflections of the Love of Source.

- Let us use our voice as a beacon of benevolent truthfulness to create beauty and a heavenly reality as we sing the songs of Remembrance.

- Let us hold a clear vision of harmony and peace and open ourselves to divine guidance as we project our inspired visions of Heaven on Earth.

- Let us open our minds to the Divine Light and Divine Intelligence and become a People of Light!

- We ARE the unification of Life! We are the Lovelight of Source Creator! We are infinity consciousness bliss. Right now! Right here! Forever!

Blessed be!
Aho! Amen! Jai!
Hallelujah!
We are here. We are awake. We are One.
And so, it is!
OM

ASCENSION LEXICON

I have put together a list of words commonly used in this book and for the topics of awakening, spirituality, and ascension. These are not necessarily defined this way by others but are an excellent way to understand my writings in this book in a more clear and multidimensional way.

-A-

Adamic Form: Original perfected divine human form created for highly developed Light Beings to experience physical creation from within the physical dimension. Fourth Density (4D) body of the New Earth human connecting with oversoul consciousness, higher dimensional beings, and telepathic species.

Agartha: Ancient Inner Earth multi-species civilization with its own sun and ecosystem within the Earth. See *Inner Earth.*

Ain Soph: Kabbalistic term for Source before manifestation into form and translates to "Without Limit" as it is the unlimited creative potential behind all of Creation. Same as "Ineffable" in the Gnostic texts. Can also be written as "Ensof."

Akashic records: Higher-dimensional spiritual records of all experience past, present, and future. Each soul has one. So does each planet and so on.

alchemy: The application of spiritual knowledge to matter to create transformation. This is more commonly known with the Middle Ages' pursuits of turning simple metals into gold. High alchemy being the alchemy of soul/lightbody.

Ancient Egypt: Last golden age of Gaia when many beings held 4th, 5th, and 6th-dimensional consciousness before the descent into lower consciousness (forgetting).

Andromedans: Highly advanced star beings from the Andromeda galaxy assisting humanity's ascension.

Anunnaki: Star beings from the Nibiru system. Sumerian space "gods" who manipulated humanity for personal gain. Now most are in support of humanity's ascension.

apocalypse: 1. Greek word for "unveiling." 2. The dismantling of the mind control matrix and false projections from the controlling forces to reveal to humanity the ugly underbelly and karma of the collective consciousness upon the Earth from this creation cycle which is to be fully reconciled before the planet changes in dimension to Fourth Density New Earth. Not the "end" but a transitionary phase into the next creation cycle.

Archons/Controllers: Term used to describe negatively polarized service-to-self, nonphysical, intelligent beings who siphon negative energy from humanity for their own gain using mind control tactics to keep humanity enslaved through fear and distorted consciousness. The controlling forces behind global institutions. Will be fully dismantled before the shift to New Earth.

Arcturians: Star beings from the constellation of Arcturus assisting Earth with Ascension.

Ascension/ascension: 1. The spiritual maturity process of a soul, moving from an unawakened state of mundane consciousness to multidimensional Source/God-realization described as the movement of the kundalini up the central channel, samadhi, moksha, nirvana, salvation... 2. The movement of Creation into greater states of Glory. 3. The current collective planetary transformation from 3D to 5D consciousness and the New Earth reality.

ascension symptoms: Physical, etheric, mental, and spiritual changes during ascension cycles. Includes headaches, emotional purging, detoxifications symptoms, multidimensional DNA reprogramming, body aches, vivid dreams, and beyond.

Ascended Master: Level of spiritual hierarchy of beings who have ascended in their consciousness enough to no longer need to incarnate in form for spiritual growth but may choose to incarnate to assist the ascension process of a species.

Atman: Divine origin identity, True Self, True Nature, the Witness Consciousness of a lifestream. Same as Brahman. Source Self. Eternally free.

aura: Electromagnetic field of subtle energy that surrounds and pervades the physical body. Contains ever-shifting patterns and geometries of light and vibration that create the template for the physical form.

-B-

biotransducer: organic instrument for transforming energy information for the purpose of manifestation and communication with the universal hologram and divine frequencies. Able to utilize advanced intelligence and spiritual information for the transformation of reality in the human environment.

bodhisattva: Sanskrit term for someone on the path of Buddhahood (ascension) who dedicates their path to the liberation of all beings from cycles of suffering. Able to achieve liberation but delays to assist others in consciousness expansion.

Brahman: The Absolute Reality. Source in impersonal, nonmanifest state. Pure Infinity Existence Consciousness Bliss, *Satchitananda*.

buddhi: the Intellect, reflected consciousness, enlightened consciousness in each person.

buddhic consciousness: enlightened consciousness expressed by *buddhi*, the vehicle for the soul, experienced as profound intuitive insight, unity, and bliss.

-C-

Cabal: Global elite network of negatively polarized service-to-self operatives and organizations working towards complete domination of humanity and planet Earth. See *Archons.*

causal consciousness: the higher mind capacity which utilizes soul memory and intuition to observe and understand manifestation multidimensionally.

centering: Alignment with one's divine nature and inner truth, activating a bridge between Gaia and the Divine through the heart center.

centropy: Regenerative electrification of matter-energy.

chakras: Spiraling transformers of subtle energy with seven primary vortices emanating from the central channel (*sushumna*) which govern our perception of the projected holographic reality and energize our mental and physical processes.

channeling: Opening one's consciousness and vessel as a conduit for subtle energy or other consciousnesses.

Christ: 1. Yeshua ben Joseph (Jesus) in his ascended Lightbody. Forerunner of christ consciousness as part of a divine plan for redemption and restoration of humanity and Earth back to a 4th Density collective. 3. A collective consciousness field that has many emanations and incarnated forms throughout the history of Creation. 4. Title given to one who has achieved consciousness mastery and is "anointed" by Light.

christ consciousness: Also called cosmic consciousness or 5D consciousness. Demonstrated by Jesus of Nazareth in his resurrected 4th Density body.

Christ/Magdalene Lineage: Genetic implantation of higher DNA coding through the offspring of Jesus and Mary. Descendants are worldwide and able to carry a higher light quotient and awaken more easily.

clairaudience: Clear hearing is the ability to hear messages from your Higher Self or spirit beings. This includes hearing the thoughts of other people.

clairgustance: Clear tasting is the ability to receive intuitive information through the sense of taste.

clairesalience: Clear smelling is the ability to intuit information through the sense of smell.

clairvoyance: Clear sight is the ability to perceive information through internal imagery.

clear channeling: Mediumship, or spirit channeling, is the ability to communicate with nonphysical beings and consciousness structures. This can include souls who have passed beyond the veil of physical life or beings that exist in other dimensions.

collective: Representing an entire group, i.e., human collective.

Collective Messiahship: The unification of ascending humanity with the intention of global restoration and ascendency.

cords: Subtle energy attachments that connect us to other beings. Can be negative if developed through limiting beliefs and distorted conditioning.

council: Group of beings joined together with a common focus (i.e., your spiritual council of guides who support your spiritual maturation across lifetimes).

Councils of Light: Groups of advanced spiritual beings that govern the evolution of consciousness and the biological forms of a certain experimental zone to encourage higher states of glory and harmony with the highest being the Universal Council of Light.

-D-

density: 1. Mass per volume. 2. Bandwidth of consciousness reality.

Descension/descension: To go down. The forgetting or falling asleep phases of consciousness. The stepping down of light frequency.

dharma: The noble path of awakening guided through alignment with the Divine through one's True Nature. Exemplified by the life path of beings like Jesus and the Buddha.

The Divine: The frequency emanation that governs and sustains all of Creation across many universes within universes. God Source and the Hosts of Heaven. See *Godhead*.

Divine Androgyny: Harmonic synergy between the divine masculine and divine feminine energetic expressions that results in perfect balance and cohesion.

Divine Creatorship: The birthright of a human to create their life with free-will choice in alignment with their Inner Source.

Divine Feminine: 1. Nurturing creative quality of the Divine 2. Archetypal, spiritual, and psychological ideal of the feminine energetic expression.

Divine Masculine: 1. Administrative quality of the Divine 2. Archetypal, spiritual, and psychological ideal of the masculine energetic expression.

DNA: Genetic blueprint for the development of an organism with both physical and subtle components. Ascended humanity will have 12 fully restored strands.

-E-

Earth Changes: Physical and subtle energetic changes that occur on the planet as it prepares to shift into the next creation cycle. Includes pole shifts, weather changes, seismic and volcanic activity, electromagnetic shifts, and more.

Elohim: First Creation. Creator beings with individual consciousness that work in groups to form Creation. Some created as service-to-all working in unity with Source. Some were created as service-to-self permitted to create in the illusion that they were separate from Source.

empath: Individual who is sensitive to the subtle energy such as thought, and emotional projections of others as they intuitively feel the mental/emotional body of others within their own mental/emotional realm. See *clairsentience*.

End Times: The closing of this current creation cycle where all karma must be balanced, and all shadow revealed so that Earth and spiritually activated humanity can begin the next creation cycle in 4th Density New Earth. See *apocalypse*.

energy: Subtle energy beyond the visible light spectrum ranging from pervasive to neutral to regenerative and life-enhancing. Everything is energy.

energy awareness: Perception of subtle energy in and around one's body.

energy matrix: Geometric organization of subtle frequencies that creates the base structure for the development of form.

entity attachment: Astral debris that has attached itself to a weakened energy system of a host as a source of sustenance and a way to live out "unfinished business." Quite common and easily resolved most of the time by a trained spirit releasement practitioner or energy medicine practitioner.

entropy: Decay and degeneration of matter-energy.

extraterrestrial: From outside of the Earth's biosphere including other planets and universes. There are countless species in our solar system, galaxy, super galaxy, and beyond. Infinite species in infinite realms of creation with many advanced civilizations with histories tracing back trillions of years.

evolution: See *Higher Evolution.*

-F-

false prophets: Teachers and prophets who use spiritual information for service-to-self agendas. Many religious leaders, spiritual teachers, and even those in the ascension community will have their true intentions revealed in the final phases of Ascension.

Family of Light: Physical and nonphysical beings who live their lives in alignment with the Oneness of Creation and the Divine Source. Includes the races of the Star Nations who hold 5D consciousness and higher and the Hierarchy of Light who tend to the many levels of Light Creation.

5D: Consciousness of humans living on the New Earth, can be referred to as christ consciousness or oversoul consciousness.

4D: Awakening stage of ascension bridging mundane consciousness with the New Earth consciousness.

frequency: 1. Rate of vibration measured in hertz (Hz). 2. Higher vibrational rate is likened to positivity and centropy and lower rate towards negativity and entropy.

-G-

Gaia: 1. Sentient Earth 2. Common name for the soul of Earth. Also called Terra.

Galactic Federation of Light: Intergalactic and ultraterrestrial collective of advanced beings who tend to the evolution of consciousness and biological forms throughout the Milky Way. Comprised of advanced scientists, engineers, medical personnel, and other areas of expertise needed to maintain order and balance in the galaxy.

genetic implantation: Seeding of new DNA into the gene pool to evolve a species into higher states of harmony or functionality. Used by the Star Nations and Hierarchy of Light to craft zones of biological experimentation.

gnosis: Direct experience of divine nature through one's own inner being and inner knowing that leads to higher understanding of the nature of the divine reality. See *Knowledge.*

Great Central Sun: Source of all levels of creation in this universe. Brings higher evolutionary coding from Divine Source into other central suns in the universal grid which flow to each solar system evolving each region in accordance with a Divine Plan for Higher Evolution. See *Ishawara.*

Great Divide: The bifurcation of consciousness amongst humanity during the end phases of the planetary ascension process. Includes physical movement across the Earth as humanity moves to be with others of shared consciousness and similar vibration and soul path. Two-world-spit of those who hold negatively polarized, service-to-self consciousness and those of positively polarized, service-to-all consciousness.

Great White Brotherhood: More accurately **Great White Siblinghood**. Ascended Masters, human and non-human, of all gender expressions organized into different orders or councils who tend to the evolution of consciousness and sometimes incarnate to bring new teachings and new energy. Many of these Ascended Masters have aspects of themselves on the planet now to assist the Ascension.

Greys: Extraterrestrial beings from Zeta Reticuli.

God: 1. Supreme Source of Creation 2. Divine Masculine, administrative quality of Godhead, Eternal Mind. See *Ishwara.*

Goddess: 1. Divine Feminine, nurturing, regenerative, creative aspect of the Godhead. 3. Mother God.

Godhead: The Divine Consciousness Source and its various emanations and functions.

Golden Ages: Times of high consciousness and harmony upon the Earth during the Precession of the Equinoxes. (e.g., Avalon, Lemuria)

grounding: The anchoring of one's physical and subtle bodies into the Earth's core through intention, diaphragmatic breathing, and visualization through the Root and Earth Star chakras.

guides: Spiritual beings who assist an incarnated being on their dharmic path towards liberation.

-H-

hara line: Central pillar of light connecting an individual with Gaia and Source.

heart-centered: Action born from inner truth and spiritual ethics through alignment with one's divine nature.

Hierarchy of Light: Various levels of divine consciousness forms, aspects of Source that serve different functions in the evolution of Creation. Ain Soph/Source, Elohim, Archangels, Angelic Realm, Ascended Masters, Ascended Goddesses, Interdimensional Beings, and Restored Humanity in Adamic Form. The Hosts of Heaven.

Higher Evolution: Beyond biological evolution and natural selection, the recoding of experimental zones of the hologram of Creation using divinely encoded frequencies projected through the stellar network which are coordinated by benevolent beings, physical and nonphysical, who serve the evolution of the Divine Plan throughout the Multiverse. Also includes introduction of new genetic expressions into the gene pool, new technologies, and new ideas to be used to evolve the creation into higher order.

Higher Self: 1. The mature part of our consciousness which operates in positively polarized, service-to-all consciousness and is connected to our divine nature. 2. Sovereign self. 3. Harmonic Divine/Human synthesis. 4. Oversoul. 5. Atman.

Holding space: A term used in spiritual growth and self-development circles that means "to hold suffering in an alchemical container of loving awareness so that it may heal."

Holy Spirit Shekinah: The feminine regenerative energy of the Divine. The "presence of God" in the physical dimension. Opening yourself to channel the divine presence begins an alchemical process of light activation that heals and restores all levels of one's being.

-I-

Inner Earth: Ancient and contemporary subterranean civilizations. Many beings went to Inner Earth before the destruction of Lemuria and

Atlantis. See *Agartha*.

intention: Inner resolve to direct one's focus and creative capacity towards a specific goal. *Sankalpa* in Sanskrit.

interdimensional: Existing between dimensions.

intuition: The ability to perceive energy information beyond the five senses before it has become physically manifested in reality. 2. Extrasensory perception.

involution: spiritual consciousness activation that begins as one moves through Ascension and sheds the mind's conditioning.

Ishwara: 1. personal expression of Source. 2. Source in purest manifested form. Commonly called "God" 3. Great Central Sun. 4. Universal Logos.

-J-

Jesus/Yeshua ben Joseph: Master of Light for Earth. Twin flame of Mary Magdalene. Supreme teacher of Divine Love and Ascension. Brought restored DNA and pure Christ Light to the Earth to activate the 4th Density Redemption Plan. Yeshua's cosmic oversoul legacy includes many star systems including the high spiritual schools of Light in the Pleiades and Sirius A and B. His arrival into this dimension of space was the Star of Bethlehem Lightship. His life path was supported by many galactic beings incarnated upon the Earth as well as many extraterrestrials and ultraterrestrial beings. 2. Incarnation of Ascended Master Lord Sananda.

-K-

karma: 1. The sum of a being's actions in this life and in previous existences, both positive and negative actions which influences the soul's path through incarnations.

Knowledge: "Gnosis," divine insight that activates higher consciousness and God-realization. Sanskrit *aparoksha*

kundalini: Serpentine energy originating at the base of the spine that ascends through the sushumna during the awakening process creating ecstatic spiritual expression.

-L-

Lemuria: First advanced human civilization. Often associated with the Pacific Ocean. Destroyed by major flooding and earth changes.

ley lines: Subtle energy pathways that carry evolutionary information across the planetary grid. Also called dragon lines, songlines, telluric lines.

Light: Regenerative divine energy emanations that exist beyond the typical visible light spectrum (Holy Spirit). Different than conventional light from lightbulbs.

Light beings: 1. General term for nonphysical beings of divine origin. See *Family of Light.*

lightbody: 1. subtle body 2. Vital, lower, and higher mind sheaths. 3. Transmigrating soul

Light Conception: The act of conceiving a child directly from the spiritual realms without the need of sperm from a physical being.

Light language: 1. Language spoken through connection to the Divine Presence. Activates multidimensional healing and powerful internal experiences with healing frequencies. Gift of the Holy Spirit, the regenerative creative frequency that quickens and restores all levels of Life. Can be self-initiated or pushed through from the Higher Self and the Divine.

Light Seed: Higher-dimensional, light-encoded genetic material used for Light Conception and altering the genetic composition of a species. Aka *Immaculate Conception.*

Lightship/lightship: Divine craft made by one individual's lightbody/merkaba or a merged merkaba from more than one being for the purpose of interdimensional travel through space-time, stargates, and higher light realms.

Love: Beyond egoic love, unconditional love that is naturally expressed when one develops love for the divine and a service-to-all intention. *Agape* love.

lokas: Sanskrit word for the planes of existence.

loosh: energy of suffering and death harvested by negative human, extraterrestrial, and interdimensional beings which is used to fuel nefarious agendas.

Lyrans: Star beings from the constellation of Lyra. Most commonly known race is the feline beings. First humanoid race in the Milky Way. Original 144,000 oversoul starseeds to bring the human species to Earth.

-M-

magic(k): Use of universal, natural law, and intention to manifest. Can be either service-to-self (dark) or service-to-all (light).

manifestation: The materialization of intention into form.

mantra: Holy names and phrases repeatedly spoken or thought which generate divine thoughtforms to reprogram the physical, etheric, and mental bodies opening one's consciousness to higher perception, divine insight, and union with the Divine. Use of mantra repatterns the DNA, clearing distortion and debris and reprogramming it into higher order and functionality for the projection of divine consciousness light.

Mary Magdalene: Twin Flame and Divine Partner of Jesus. Ancient Egyptian Priestess. High initiate from the Pleiades, Venus, and other high consciousness realms. Arrived at Earth with Yeshua in the Star of Bethlehem Lightship. Gave birth to the offspring of Jesus. This lineage is spread throughout the world.

maya: Illusion. Projecting and veiling power of Source. All that has form and name which tests our ability to see the all-pervasive divine consciousness that supports all manifestations.

meditation: Conscious focusing of the mind on a single object.

merkaba: Divine light vehicle in the auric field that gives one the ability to travel to the higher light realms. Introduced back to humanity through Elijah.

Michael: Archangel who protects and defends all levels of Creation and biological life.

mindfulness: The practice of bringing our life's gross and subtle manifestations into the light of our awareness to observe life in nonduality. Nondual awareness is the ability to see beyond the illusion of duality and see with the eyes of loving awareness.

Mother Mary: Cosmic divine being, a Master soul, who incarnated to give birth to Jesus. High priestess of Ancient Egypt and master teacher of the cosmic priestess arts.

multidimensional: Existing in multiple planes of consciousness, i.e., physical, etheric, mental, and various spiritual dimensions.

Multiverse/multiverse: Universes within universes creating the totality of Creation. What Jesus spoke of when he referred to his "Father's house with many mansions."

-N-

nadis: Pathways of subtle energy in the body. There are said to be 72,0000 that weave in and around the physical body.

New Earth: 1. Higher density light spectrum reality of the ascended Earth. 2. Kingdom of Heaven on Earth.

nirvanic consciousness: liberated consciousness which has transcended suffering, limited egoic identity, and karmic cycles.

-O-

Orion: Constellation with ancient intelligent races with varying levels of consciousness and ranges of polarity. Factions of Reptilian and humanoid beings from Orion fought against Lyrans in the long galactic war.

oversoul: Higher consciousness identity of a soul. Where your individual soul comes from. Collective consciousness of myriad life streams and incarnations. 4th Density/5D Self.

-P-

past life regression: Form of hypnosis or shamanic journeying that evokes information from a client's subconscious mind from previous lifetimes.

Pleiadians: Star beings from the constellation of Pleiades, a highly advanced light consciousness school in our great universe. Cousins of humanity. They implanted upgraded DNA in humanity to open our spiritual connection.

prayer: Approach to the Divine through thought or word which opens the pathways for the living Light to infuse the one who is praying with love and divine insight.

priest: Male devotee of the Divine in service to the illumination of collective consciousness and the ascension of humanity. Administers the will and knowledge of the divine upon the Earth as well as the regenerative, healing presence of the divine feminine.

priestess: Female devotee of the Divine. Often connected to the Goddess. Embodies the wisdom of the divine feminine mothering principle of the Godhead. Matures consciousness in the community into higher states of creativity, sensuality, and grace.

psychic: One who has extrasensory perception. See *intuition*.

pyramids: Sacred architectural sites around the Earth built by various extraterrestrial and ultraterrestrial beings connecting the pathways of vital energy of the Earth with the universal energy grid for the reprogramming of life upon planet Earth. Act as broadcast and receiving systems for information used for planetary evolution.

Prakriti: Manifested reality, transactional reality as opposed to Absolute Reality, maya.

Purusha: Indwelling witness of Creation, Absolute Reality, Brahman, Pure Consciousness. Source Consciousness.

-Q-

quantum: Dealing with the holographic reality and fabric of Consciousness and creation.

quantum consciousness: Holographic consciousness connecting to the matrix of Creation with the ability to focus across time and space through nonlocality and consciousness projection.

quantum healing: Rapid, multidimensional healing that works at the cellular and subtle levels to bring the body's systems into homeostasis. Can be done through psychic processes, shamanic and energy medicine practices, hypnosis, quantum healing technology, star technology, and divine emanations. This is the medicine of New Earth.

quantum mysticism: Emerging evolutionary synthesis between science, metaphysics, and spirituality used to understand Consciousness and the laws that govern Creation.

Qumran: Ancient, multigenerational esoteric Essene community by the Dead Sea in present-day Israel that lived in complete recognition of the Divine through the study and embodiment of divine mystery teachings. Secretive community with advanced star knowledge and superhuman spiritual abilities. Traded knowledge with other global mystery schools and was home and school to Yeshua, Jesus of Nazareth. Yeshua's children studied here as well.

-R-

Reiki: 1. Japanese word meaning spiritual intelligence life force. 2. Intelligently-encoded, divine, redemptive, and regenerative energy from Source. 3. A gift of the Holy Spirit.

Redemption Plan: Cosmic and galactic initiative to restore humanity and Earth back to 4th Density as in the times of Lemuria. Includes genetic implantation, restoration of planetary grid, and operatives incarnating as human to bring new ideas and technologies, broadcasting intelligent and spiritual coding into the biofield of Earth and humanity, and more.

Reptilians: Reptilian humanoid star beings who have had a "negative" influence on Earth who have mostly evolved to positive polarity. Humans have reptilian DNA that gives us our ego mind to assist our perseverance in evolving.

reincarnation: The act of being born again into a new lifestream for the purpose of spiritual growth.

resonance: In spiritual terms, harmonic, synchronous vibrations between two or more objects.

Raphael: Archangel who administers to healing.

-S-

sacred sexuality: Alchemical sexual expression with the intention of uniting with the divine through one's own erotic spiritual nature. Can be practiced alone or with a partner(s).

sacred sites: Holy power spots spread across the planet that form a web of vortex points for subtle energy pathways of the Earth.

samsara: 1. Wheel of Karma 2. rounds and rounds of incarnations on the path of Ascension 3. Suffering mind. 4. Cycles of suffering.

samskaras: Grooves in the mind that create reactive emotions forming our biases, habits, and tendencies. Can be seen as negative or positive.

Self: Divine Self as opposed to the egoic self which is trapped in worldly conditioning.

sentience: The ability to feel, be conscious, or have one's own subjective experience.

service-to-all: Positively polarized, dedicated intention, thought, and action towards the Greater Good and Higher Love as an extension of one's True Self.

service-to-self: Negatively polarized, gives power to false self, ego. Can seem "positive" as intentions can be different than presentation.

sin: Intention, thought, and action that goes against one's inner light that causes an immediate depletion of life force and positive vibration. Serves the egoic self. There is no judgment for this from higher realms. All is for learning and growth. 2. Fear-based judgment system created by religion which connects to belief systems that limit the indwelling of spiritual light by creating perpetual states of fear, shame, and guilt. 3. The fundamental illusion of separation from Source.

Sirians: Star beings from the region of the Sirius A and Sirius B binary star system who have a long, positive history with humanity and are assisting Earth now.

Solaris: Central sun and stargate of our solar system which emanates supraliminal coding for the evolution of the myriad lifeforms in our solar system.

soul: 1. Subtle bodies which transmigrate from one life to the next. See *lightbody.*

spiritual partnership: A relationship that is supported by the desire to assist one another in awakening and healing.

soul contracts: Pre-designed plan and agreements before incarnating for the balancing of karma to propel the path of liberation and ascension. Includes soul agreements between individual souls to play out certain catalyst roles.

soul purpose: Divine intention for a soul for its incarnation encompassing the themes to be explored and lessons to be learned throughout a lifestream. Generally, a soul's purpose is to awaken to Higher Love and Divine Truth.

sovereign: natural consciousness state of the Atman/Self/Inner Source. Human beings embody and reclaim sovereignty through involution and higher consciousness evolution. Able to have agency in all areas of life. Self-regulated. Self-governed.

stargate: Portal used for transportation between long distances and different dimensions.

Star Nations: Space-traveling intelligent species, some positive, some negative, some neutral in relation to humanity and the Earth.

starseeds: Visitors from other schools in the multiverse who have volunteered to live a human life to assist the Ascension of Gaia and humanity. Many of which have experienced ascension mastery in other lifetimes. The best ascension masters from the universe are here on the planet or around the planet in crafts at this time.

substratum: 1. Foundational, base material 2. Source/Brahman/Atman/Pure Consciousness.

superluminal: 1. faster than light

synchronicity: The meeting of two or more seemingly unrelated events or objects that come together in a meaningful way that could even be perceived as divinely coordinated.

-T-

timelines: Pathways of probable events. Infinite potentials and realities fractal out and converge at particular junction points in "time" where choice points exist for the next fractal offshoots of timeline potentials. We are currently moving with multiple timeline potentials for Ascension events that lead to one inevitable event, 4th/5th Density New Earth. Timelines are constantly in flux depending on personal moment-to-moment choices from individuals or the collective meaning the future is never "fixed" but is always in flux. This is the reason why some psychics see different potential probabilities playing out in the future.

3D: Standard human consciousness in its unawakened state, fear/duality-based consciousness which is heavily programmed and hypnotized by the false matrix, the conditioning of the world, and the mind control techniques from the Archons.

Elders: Highest divine council. Progenitors of all cultures in the multiverse.

Twin Flames: Emanations of the same oversoul who assist one another in Ascension. Often uniting at the end of karmic cycles to serve Consciousness. Most commonly thought of as two people in Divine Partnership, but there can be more.

-U-V-W-Y-

Unified Field: The hologram of Creation, the Quantum Field, where all energies and manifestations arise from connecting all through Source Consciousness.

ultraterrestrial: Beings from beyond the physical plane, higher density beings in higher density forms.

vibration: The invisible, subtle layers of matter that form the basic templates for physical reality through repetitive oscillation.

Wisdom: Insight into the Divine Mysteries of Creation and the Godhead that connects us with higher states of divine love and divine grace. See *Knowledge, gnosis.*

walk-in: Exchange of souls during an incarnation. Typically occurs when the original soul consciousness assigned to the body can no longer continue an incarnation from trauma or some other way of vital depletion. A fresh soul consciousness is brought in to accomplish a certain task. Frequently used to bring highly developed galactic beings into the Earth for mission-oriented tasks.

Yeshua ben Joseph: See *Jesus* and *Christ*.

Recommended Reading

The Three Waves of Volunteers and The New Earth by Dolores Cannon

They Walked with Jesus by Dolores Cannon

Jesus and the Essenes by Dolores Cannon

Between Death and Life by Dolores Cannon

Keepers of The Garden by Dolores Cannon

Five Lives Remembered by Dolores Cannon

Return of the Bird Tribes by Ken Carey

Anna: Grandmother of Jesus by Claire Heartsong

Light on Life by B.K.S. Iyengar

The Yoga Sutras of Patanjali (many translations available)

Living Buddha, Living Christ by Thich Nhat Hahn

Reconciliation: Healing the Inner Child by Thich Nhat Hahn

Peace is Every Step by Thich Nhat Hahn

The Path of Energy by Dr. Synthia Andrews

The Seat of the Soul by Gary Zukav

The Book of Knowing and Worth by Paul Selig

The Diamond in Your Pocket by Gangaji

The Magdalen Manuscript: The Alchemies of Horus & the Sex Magic of Isis by Tom Kenyon and Judi Sion

The Kybalion by Three Initiates

Aparokshanubhuti by Adi Shankara

The Upanishads

The Bhagavad Gita

Drig Drishya Viveka

The Keys of Enoch by J.J. Hurtak

Pistis Sophia translated by J.J. Hurtak

The Secret Doctrine by H.P. Blavatsky

Etheric Double by A.E. Powell

The Causal Body and the Ego by A.E. Powell

Regression: Past-life Therapy for Here and Now by Samuel Sagan

Entity Possession: Freeing the Energy Body of Negative Influences by Samuel Sagan

THE ILLUMINATION CODEX

WWW.NEWEARTHASCENDING.ORG

Support Our Initiatives

Ron and I have dedicated our lives to supporting this Grand Transition. We stand alongside all of you as humanity awakens to its True Nature and becomes a People of Light in the heavenly reality of New Earth.

New Earth Ascending is dedicated to assisting people to realize their divinity and manifest that truth in every aspect of their life. For more information about New Earth Ascending or to contact Michael, please scan the QR code below for a list of resources and links, or visit *www.newearthascending.org*. Be sure to check out our courses including the Illuminated Quantum Healing practitioner course.

New Earth Ascending is a registered 508 (c)(1)(a) Self-Supported Non-profit Church Ministry with a global outreach. We greatly appreciate your support as we create new systems, communities, and schools for the development of the New Earth civilization. If you would like to make a tax-deductible donation to support our mission, please go to:

https://donorbox.org/donationtonewearthascending

Scan with a smart device camera for more information including websites, social media, and more! Bless us all!